## Dedications

We are truly and daily blessed if we realize that life's most beautiful gifts are those around us.

I sincerely dedicate this book to my Queen, Karen, my Moorish princesses Alisha, Nicole, Toni, and of course my friends and brothers as well as my sons, Rashad, Taijuan, and David.

# Moorish-America's Archival Palladium

## An Exposition of Alternative Moorish-American Philosophical Thought

### Volume One

### by T. Matheno Matthews - El
#### Adept Emeritus

Moorish-America's Archival Palladium

Copyright © 2010 T. Matheno Matthews - El

CreateSpace

Nonfiction/Philosophy

First Edition (December, 2010)
First Printing (December, 2010)

Volume One

ISBN-13: 978-1456457082
ISBN-10: 145645708X

# Table of Contents

# Introduction

One of the challenges faced in writing this book, was to avoid focusing exclusively on the issues of race or to proselytize to any extent for a particular religion, but to present some philosophical observations as suggestive areas of interest, for those looking for other possibilities of thought and uses of Moorish Science. This was extremely difficult because much of the Moorish-American public doctrine deals with the problems of American's racial traditions and history.

For those reasons we introduce some of those Moorish-American teachings and theories in our historical survey, and, as they may be applied in each particular chapter, allowing the whole work to be fused into our thesis. However, there are a number of underlying ideologies, sacred teachings, and abstract concepts that synthesize the whole system of Moorish Science, though they are not readily apparent, but become perceivable in concert with the cognitive growth of the individual.

Further, in view of the Moorish leader's more prophetic statements concerning the future of Black people in this country, Prophet Drew Ali may have expected his adepts to take the initiative in acquiring, maintaining, and making available to the descendents of Africa, the knowledge and ability, to meet all Constitutional requirements, by supplying the necessary knowledge and insight that most of Black America often lacks, the things necessary to be prosperous, productive, and industrious, like other American citizens.

Therefore, through these several chapters, we present a few Moorish Science mystical postulations, spiritual observations, philosophical concepts, and literary references, intermittently, and from the premise, that Moorish Science Temple organizations, being lawfully Chartered and recognized by the free- national government of the United States of America, and around the world, to function and operate according to it's expressed and lawful parameters, owe no deference to any American or European Masonic body, secret society, mystery school or to any of their chartered authorities.

This should in no way be interpreted as ill regard or disrespect toward that or any other organization. One of Drew Ali's most pointed directives to the Moors, was that they abstain from all radical talk and that members were not to speak radically against any member of any organized group, the Prophet emphasized " *we are for peace, and not destruction* ". The failure of too many Moorish-Americans and

19

Moorish leaders, to obey those instructions and conform to the mission of uplifting themselves and their brothers and sisters, has contributed directly to the inability of our people, in this hour of greatest difficulty, to benefit from the tremendous wealth of knowledge and opportunities for spiritual, philosophical, political and economic growth, provided through the groundbreaking work of Noble Drew Ali.

Nevertheless, we are persuaded, after more than three decades of earnest inquiry, diligent study, practical application and testing of Moorish science, that there exists a wealth of previously hidden, unknown history, philosophical insight, spiritual wisdom, and the ancient keys to mystical illumination, carefully, masterfully, ensconced throughout the illustrious Noble Drew Ali's original body of work. Intuitively adduced, from his masterful compilations of esoteric literature, the selection of mystical (masonic-type) symbols, to the Moorish Temple's structure and organization, as well as the Prophet's appearance and speech used in various dissertations.

Some controversy rages, even at the present time, as to whether or not Noble Drew Ali passed through the required Masonic initiations (32nd degree), to cross the level to the mystic shrine.  If Noble Drew Ali received instructions and initiations thru inter-national bodies of Adepts, and Grand Rulers, in the interwoven systems of the ancient initiatory traditions and sacred teachings , from Fez Morocco, once the location of the " Collegum Adeptus " or College of the Adepts, to Egypt with it's lesser and greater mysteries, it's pyramidal traditions ( evidence suggests that Ali's original Charter was granted by Egypt, out of the actual Egyptian Temple ) , as well as the shrine of Arabia and the arcanum of the desert, then it is subsequently immaterial, as these venerable sources of the sacred doctrine form an uninterrupted process that pre-dates by thousands of years any western free-masonic order or mystery school.

Furthermore, it is to some of these same bodies that western free masons must look to continue their masonic education.

The mystery traditions of the sacred schools are often spoken of in the western world ( Occident ) , as opposed to the eastern lands ( Orient ) , as if they were the exclusive inheritance of only Europeans that function within the super-structure of the western free-masonic order, in which they have often describe themselves as the " custodians " of the ancient mysteries, most expressively, the wisdom and knowledge of the ( Black ) Egyptians, so that in their functions they appropriate for use or " borrow " the dress ( regalia ) , manners and customs and as Drew

Ali said, *"... imitating our forefathers, all but the olive hue they cannot get ",* and often with full knowledge concerning the true history and birthrights of the Black man in America, from whose heritage they are dependent on for the knowledge needed to maintain their own civilization, country and nation.

Therefore, we have a selected several themes with which to explore philosophically some of the basic teachings of Moorish Science, and to present as accurately as possible or permissible, some of the views or original intentions of Ali. We do not represent any group or body of Moorish-Americans and the statements within this book represent the personal observations, views and determinations of the author.

## The Archival Palladium

Crystallized, in the little known teachings and practices, of what has until recent years been an obscure, most often mis-understood religious sect, are keys to many modern and ancient systems of symbolic instruction, mystical illumination, spiritual wisdom of the eastern world, philosophical ties to contemporary and ancient sacred schools, and the true history as well as identities of many of America's African descendants. Those teachings and practices were derived from the original sources, the same from which many modern day western masonic orders trace their origins.

This religious organization, has existed in the African-American community for almost one hundred years, since its establishment in 1913. It's founding began with the work of Noble Drew Ali in Newark, New Jersey, and the opening of the Holy Canaanite Temple, for the purpose of teaching his people *" their true nationality and birthrights ",* and *"their forefather's ancient and divine creed ".*

Drew Ali, came to the people as a Prophet, who had been sent to the lost descendents of Africa, by the Great God,   Allah, to warn the African-Americans

23

( at that time called negro, black, and colored ), to abandon the sinful practices and names they had acquired while slaves, and become law-abiding citizens, leaders in their communities, business owners, entrepreneurs, well taught scholars, lovers of wisdom, spiritual people, builders of civilization as their ancient fore-fathers had been. He taught that the fall of Africa's world empires and the enslavement of millions in the west, happen because of sin and that the same type of sin must be removed from America to save it and to save it's people.

Despite his obvious sincerity, most of the American Prophet's warnings were ignored, his message lost, confused with *" radical, agitating speeches "*, and the greed and envy of unscrupulous persons.

The illustrious American Prophet was eventually to die at a young age, yet his historical work and legendary accomplishments have reverberated for decades throughout the Black experience in America. It has impacted and influenced, either directly or indirectly, practically every step of African-American progress and history, over the last one hundred years, touching numerous Black movements, Islamic, social, civil, religious and esoteric organizations since the beginning of the early 1900s.

Though the original organization and movement has

long since fractured into multiple Moorish temples with different doctrinal views and methods, and marginal participation in African American community life, if the recent and growing intensity of research and interest in Noble Drew Ali, and the teachings of his Moorish Science are any indications, the Prophet may, to some extent, realize his promise to "rise up, and walk with my people some day".

There are increasing numbers of African American writers, researchers, and scholars, who are coming forward in sincerity and humility, giving honor to the life, works, and memory of Noble Drew Ali and his Moorish Science Temple of America, extending the learning and contributing to the work. Also, all the silent brotherhood of light, most of whom have labored in obscurity, but continued to share in the great work, of uplifting fallen humanity. Whether Black, African-American, Moorish-American, or by whatever name we call ourselves, we are still a common people with a common bond.

Now approaching one hundred fifty years after our release from physical bondage, we find ourselves yet locked in a desperate battle for mere survival. We are facing real and difficult challenges in this country, though not as severe as those endured by millions of our ancestors, they are more subtle, under-handed, continuing racial disparity that operates in a more

25

indistinguishable, yet equally destabilizing manner.

Affecting this present society, with it's blurred, almost invisible  lines of separation, it's traditional avenues to prosperity and success hedged about with acknowledged familiarity and quiet consent, maintaining the centuries old customs of right, privilege and preference.

No living beings on this earth, can possibly be as tired of America's racial dilemma, as the millions of African-Americans themselves, burdened with a pressing weight that must be dealt with and dealt with every day. We go to bed with it looming over many of our lives, and not long after we get out of bed every mourning, most of us will soon encounter it in some form or another.

Most of us have no desire whatsoever to return hatred for hatred, nor to be continually subject to harassment or prejudicial treatment, but expect to obtain freedom, justice, and equality, in this, the land of our birth, and to overcome once and for all, the dark legacy of slavery and take our place in the affairs of men.

*"I bought you everything it takes to save a nation, now take it and save yourself..."*, when the
Prophet Noble Drew Ali said that,  it is reported that he was holding up a Holy Koran (circle seven) of the

Moorish Science Temple of America, and a
questionnaire

Moorish people from every walk of life come through
the doors of the temple, some are enlightened, some
disillusioned, most gather any useful knowledge and
move on to meet life's challenges, a few stay and dwell
in the temple for a lifetime, but we are persuaded very
few, if any, remain the same.

Due to the multifarious nature of Moorish science, it is
with great patience, years of diligent research,
study, meditation, practical application and
experimentation, above all else, sincerity of heart, that
if
the All-knowing God permits, one may comprehend in
a measure this ancient wisdom. The essential work of
Noble Drew Ali's Divine and National Movement,
manifested in several stages 1913-1929, nationally and
internationally, to re-orient the African-American
Community to its Afro-Asiatic origins and world-
view.

There are no steps outlined for one to travel through
the "Temple", therefore, the many books that are
becoming available highlighting different areas of
thought and investigative inquiry, are timely blessings
as *" the Moorish hordes increase here in America "*.

As with the beginnings of any religious group, philosophical, esoteric, spiritual or the like, there are at first but the fundamental ideas, beliefs, revelations, and teachings, around which a usually small core of " believers " or adherents form . These various teachings and principals are developed and recorded for future use and referenced when consideration must be given to any aspect of official doctrine or methods of operation.  A complete body of knowledge grows into a theological super structure, becoming over time the tried and tested frame of reference.

Ali was apparently fully persuaded that it was "Allah alone  that guided " the destiny " of the Moorish Temple, as well as the life of each that submitted to His will. Nevertheless, the Prophet left his foot prints clearly cut, that all with eyes to see, could know that he, their Master, went that way. The true master teacher does not lead the student to the teacher's well of wisdom, but introduces the disciple to his own well of wisdom.

In humble and sincere recognition of that masterful body of divine knowledge, manifested in the Moorish Science of the illustrious Prophet, Noble Drew Ali, we submit this work.

# Chapter One:  Historical Survey

*" The key to civilization was and is in the hands of the Asiatic Nations......The fallen sons and daughters of the Asiatic Nation of North America need to learn to love instead of hate, and to know of their higher-self and lower-self... "*

The ongoing struggle of millions of African, Hispanic, and other so-called minorities in America, to finally achieve, full freedom, justice, and equality, is far from over; it remains a problem that has not been solved, a dilemma that is yet to be decided.

But we must be crystal clear, it will be decided, and at this point in our history, what we can in the least afford to do, is to stand idly by, and ensure that the worst possible choices will be made for us.

The difficult reality may be, that we are the ultimate deciders, and are forced of necessity to question not if we have lost our way, but if we have lost our will.

In our honest opinion, we believe that, understanding the historical context, or the spiritual implications of all that we have endured in this country, and, learning to understand the why, more so than the how, may very well be the means, if not the motivational, inner fire we need, to re-energize our forward movement, to finally and emphatically, overcome.

Of course we understand how difficult and painful revisiting the past can be, but to find our answers, to understand, and to understand clearly, where we are, and how we got there, that is what we must do.

Even the collective faith, that has brought us through countless dark nights, has seemed over the past couple of decades, to have abandoned us, to have taken refuge in some distant place that we are unable to discover.

We may certainly find out, if it is always darkest before dawn, if there really is light at the end of the tunnel.

Four hundred years, says that we did not come this far for nothing, that there is an ultimate purpose and a divine plan, that it is our place, our divine appointment, to complete the journey.

Let us then, first take a quick glimpse at a good indication of where we are.

An article in a state newspaper recently, seemed

almost to pinpoint the location of Black-America. It reported the documented disparity; shockingly disproportionate punishment between " Black and White " students in one of it's public school systems, for "everything , from major to minor offenses ". If this wasn't ground zero, it was definitely the smoking gun, especially with approximately 70 percent of young Black males, dropping ( or being forced ) out of the public school systems throughout the United States each and every year, a phenomena that has continued uninterrupted for almost 30 years.

Millions of young, mostly African-American youth are efficiently, for the most, permanently removed from any possibility of participation in anything resembling normal life.

The most effective means of historically denying to African-Americans as well as other " non-whites ", the full exercise and enjoyment of all American Constitutional rights and privileges " unmolested by other citizens ", has been to undermine, distort, and frustrate any and all efforts to obtain knowledge, wisdom, and understanding. During slavery, Blacks were killed if discovered that they knew how to read, or worse how to write. In fact, even if a slave was perceived as " too smart ", educated, or " uppity ", such was quickly and publicly made an example of, to keep the others "in their places", of course meaning,

31

docile, subservient, enslaved, and defeated!

Information is knowledge, necessary, useful insight,
the " know how ", and subsequently information is
power. Theoretically, the absence or lack of power,
can be tied, indirectly at least, to the absence and lack
of knowledge, of insight, and the ability to make
prudent decisions.

Life, *free* life, is one continuous process of learning, of
growing, developing, accomplishing new things, overcoming new challenges. There must be some inner
source of inspiration, something that motivates us to
try, to do, and to achieve.

What happens when there is no inner drive, or a
person's self esteem is destroyed? What if a child is
thrown into a system that is completely foreign to their
psychological orientation, taught a history with a
social paradigm the exact opposite of themselves?
What happens when anyone is made literally from
birth to feel that they do not belong?

Such is the continuing plight of Black-America, in her
monumental and historic struggle to find her place of
victory and relevance in this 21st century. At some
point in the recent portion of our journey, we appear to
have misplaced or abandon some of the principles and
commitments that we once shared in our common

struggle.

Things that continued uninterrupted before our American history, things our fore-fathers and ancestors have always held to the highest esteem and deemed to be of the utmost importance in life, the thirst for knowledge, the quest for wisdom. We excelled in all of the known sciences at that time, taught the world, including bringing Europe out of it's millennial darkness.

To sort out some of the complexities concerning the last five centuries, especially the last four-hundred years as they apply to our history and experience in North America during that time, to place that era in an overall context as it relates to the whole of world history and civilization. The purpose being, to give us plausible answers to the questions of why, how, and what now, as we face even greater challenges in this new century.

History happens but once, yet it is recorded a thousand times and from as many perspectives. We should remember that other people, countries, and nations are not as uninformed and confused about their identity and origins as our African-American peoples have been over the last several centuries.

At the beginning of the 1900s, the entire structure of

world power was firmly in the hands of the western European nations, completing a chain of circumstances and events lasting some five-hundred years, and bringing to an end many African and Islamic empires, with the complete collapse of their combined political control and once world-wide influence.

*" ...the industrious acts of the Moslems of northwest and southwest Africa. These are the Moabites, Hamathites, Canaanites, who were driven out of the land of Canaan by Joshua, and received permission from the Pharaohs of Egypt to settle in " that " portion of Egypt. In later years they formed themselves kingdoms. These kingdoms are called this day Morocco, Algiers, Tunis, Tripoli, etc.............Through sin and disobedience every nation has suffered slavery........."*

The truth, concerning untold millions of slaves taken into brutal captivity, stripped completely of all human identity, dignity, and forced under the most vicious system of human servitude, and dehumanization ever devised on earth. To labor without compensation or consideration, denied even basic human rights they and their descendents being the unprovoked victims of a near combined four centuries of unchecked aggression and hostility, disenfranchisement, and prejudicial treatment, proves far stranger than fiction.

We may agree that having endured so much emotional pain, we are all very sensitive in this area, especially with other American citizens choosing to (insensitively) rub salt in the tender wounds. Claiming that we are now in a "post racial era", there is magically no longer any disparity, or discrimination for that matter, notwithstanding the daily evidence that suggests otherwise, they constantly infer that Black folks are just " playing the race card ".

For our people to come into knowledge concerning our true history, is to come out of a world of darkness and despair, lies, misinformation, mischaracterizing designations, hidden information, disinformation, and deceit, into a completely different reality that requires a completely different approach, an entirely different mentality.

Though some feelings of anger, depression, amazement, etc. are normal, they can be completely counterproductive, and the generally expected, in fact, the welcomed response.  It is therefore senseless, to react to the challenges that face all of us by getting angry and burning down our own houses.

What is not the expected or desired response, by those

who fear Black-America's resurrection and restoration, is that we instead act with intelligence, come into the knowledge of the truth, shake off the lower expectations, and summon the will, activate the power, and initiate the process that will raise us from the dead level.

The challenge for today's African American man, is to stand immovable, equal and erect; a man among men,"upright, independent and fearless". To inspire our young people to take up the challenge of standing shoulder to shoulder with any other nation on earth and aspire to reach new heights and to set higher standards in every noble area of endeavor and inquiry worthy of note.

If Black men recognize their responsibility, step up to the plate and be men, not cower, but insist on our rights and our rights to be, we must first and foremost be dedicated to understanding the truth, about who we are and who our ancestors were, then committing ourselves to being a part of the uplifting of our individual selves, our families, and our communities.

1492: significant for us too!

We must be as brief as possible in this area, we need not get tangled up in the issues of history no more than we wish to get lost in America's so-called definitions or concepts of race.

The year of 1492, generally seems to have less than a passing interest for African American people, being usually associated with Columbus and the European discovery of the western continents.
But the year 1492, correctly and clearly understood, holds the most profound and historic implications for African-American people and their unique places in the flow of western expansion and history over the last five centuries.

Unknown, to the vast majority of Black America, is the fact, that in that year, 1492, at Granada Spain the last of their direct ancestors' Moorish kingdoms, fell to the Spanish and European powers under King Ferdinand and Queen Isabella.

It was the end of an empire, ruled by the Islamic, Arab influenced kingdom of Moorish North Africa, that had invaded Spain in 711 and once extended it,s influence from Egypt west to Fez Morocco, south of the Sahara and according to the teachings of Noble Drew Ali and some references found in the degrees of Mystic masonry, " Across the great Atlantis, even to the present North, South, and Central America ".  An etymological study of the word ' Moor ', suggests it to be an inclusive, ancestral, cultural designation, referring to historical, family, cultural and tribal ties, rather than merely any Islamic practitioner as western historians usually write.

From 711 AD. to at least the early portions of the 1400s, Moorish tribes, whether the fierce Berbers who, with the one-eyed Moorish general, Tariq, led the original invasion onto European soil, or the Almorivdes, fanatical dark skinned warriors out of the southern Sahara, who took over the empire, established their capital at Marrakesh and ruled the Spanish lands in the early 1100s, all of those even to the extreme of south-west Africa were Moorish.

Moorish universities and libraries were among the best in the world at the time, the philosophical and scientific works, medical journals and religious literature of previous civilizations were translated into Arabic, studied and expounded upon. Advances were made in areas of chemistry, mathematics, physics, and traveling teachers, sages, mystics and philosophers were in such abundance, that they traveled, not only Africa, Arabia, and the East, but as early as the eight hundreds throughout the continent of Europe as well, instructing students and buildings schools.

History proves this to be the shadowy origins of many western secret societies and Masonic type orders that began as small circles of philosophers and mystics

participated in the transmission of Eastern and African
sacred wisdom and secret sciences.

After leading a civilized world, it was the last true
African empire, and its fall beginning with a surrender
of the kingdom of Granada, intensified with the
expulsion of hundreds of thousands of Moorish people
from every area on the Iberian Peninsula.

Portugal expelled every Moor from within its borders
into 1249, Spain follow in 1609, after the cruel
inquisition, which began in 1492, failed after more
than a century, to " cure the Moriscos of their African
ways ", or to convert them into the Roman Catholic
Church.

Every man, woman, and child of Moorish ancestry
was driven off of the peninsula, across the straits of
Gibraltar onto the coast of Africa. Suspected by many
of their kinsmen of being converts to Christianity,
untold numbers of them were sold into slavery, others
were killed.

A remarkable time with those years, 1609 to 1615,
hundreds of thousands of Moorish people seemingly
disappear into the mists of history.

Spanish, English, Dutch, French, and Portuguese
explorers ventured for the first time across the great

Atlantic Ocean, founding colonies, defeating the native populations, exploiting the resources throughout North, South and Central America.

The European nations began a period of enlightenment and awakening, called the renaissance (rebirth). From France to Scotland, England and Ireland, Moorish, Arabic and even Persian scholars, philosophers, teachers, sages, and mystics, were free to travel across the European continent to teach and educate.

For 800 years, the Moorish empire and culture ruled some portion of European lands. African and Arab knowledge and learning in the arts and sciences influenced, refined, and educated the nobles, the elite and the wealthy all across Europe to such an extent, they are probably more responsible for ending it's thousand year intellectual slumber than anything else.

During the millennial rule of the Moorish nations, Europe experience what was called "the dark ages", when almost 99% of the population were illiterate, and it was most commonly believed among themselves, that the earth was flat, while the Africans, Indians, Arabs, and Chinese, had sailed and charted most of the world.

Europe began its  ascendancy to power and world empire in that pivotal year of 1492, the discovery of gold and other valuable resources in the new world, quickly increased the wealth of exploring and colonizing European nations, filling their treasuries and igniting the Reformation.

Throughout the 1500s French, Spanish, Dutch, British and other European nations invested also in African resources, as well as slaves to work in the same type of exploitation and "colonization" that was taking place at the same time and in very similar fashion in the Americas.

By 1609, many of the former African kingdoms and powers were being brought under the attack of colonizing powers, established, operated, and controlled by European nations.
Moorish slaves from all over the north and western areas of Africa, began the flow of captured and enslaved people to North America, where they would literally be used to build " the greatest nation on Earth" ..

It is our duty and responsibility to recover our fore-father's vast estate.....it is none other than our own responsibility to see that our own history, our true history, that it is accurately documented and made available to all who have a vested interest in obtaining such knowledge.

What too many blacks have often misinterpreted about other African-American people, trying to do what it takes for them to survive, as " acting white ", may just be acting free.

We may be forced to change our perception of education, of knowledge, of getting training and becoming proficient in different areas, in order to put our children, our households in a position better to not only survive but to thrive in a rapidly evolving and changing society.

We all have enough intelligence to look at the changing world around us and understand the effect of the changes that are taking place in this country and around the world.  We know that we are in a time of astounding and phenomenal changes in technology and different forms of information systems.  The microcomputer is becoming more essential in many areas of life and it is conceivable that within a very few years, basic computer literacy will be an absolute requirement to engage in normal daily activities involving work, handling of business affairs, and perhaps most importantly, the ability to acquire information and knowledge necessary to survive period!

With those things in mind we should more easily appreciate the seriousness of our situation and understand that the most important investment in the coming age will be in the area of intellectual capital ( knowledge ) , and in that very order, the ability to access necessary and vital information, and at the speed of thought.

We cannot afford to continue to allow our children to be influenced by a completely distorted, twisted, debilitating, understanding of why they need some form of usable education, why it is necessary for them to acquire information and training that will allow them to be able to live a better life, take advantage of more opportunities, to interact on an intelligent level with the rest of the more than six billion people on earth.

A serious question for Black-America is, will we, in all of our diversity, focus our energies and resources on this final and ultimate challenge, will we step up and perform, or , will we choose rather to continue on the present course, which, by the combination of several dominating, devastating issues we are all to well familiar with, will ensure that the millions of our people will be surgically removed from the human family.

Not that we have to confine our children or ourselves to " the public fool system ", there are ever increasing alternative ways of building our knowledge base and we need to invest and support our own community schools and charter schools, religious schools and private training facilities. We can in no way afford to be disillusioned or mistaken, we cannot remain in a state of inertia, and until Black-America becomes again an energized, focused, cohesive unit, there can be no significant overall progress, in what has been for four hundred years, an intense struggle to obtain freedom, justice and equality in America.

## Chapter Two:   A New World View

In light of the information revealed in the preceding chapter, we have to completely reassessed everything that we had previously believed to be true, historically, religiously, socially, economically, even our personal view of ourselves, everything must be reassessed, re-evaluated, and placed in the proper perspectives.

This may cause us, perhaps for the first time in our lives, to see many things and understand many things, from entirely different points of view.  When we can see things differently we can find alternative ways of approaching or dealing with them.

*" ...if I can get you to think, you can save yourself... "*
*( attributed to Noble Drew Ali )...." We must believe*
*in the capacity of our group to succeed "*

We need to not get rid of our desire, but focus and concentrate those powers into different and more beneficial directions.

One Greek philosopher is said to have taken a student who desired knowledge out waist deep into the water and then asked him, " what do you want more than

anything in the world?", to which the student is said to have replied," knowledge". The teacher then grabbed him by his head, pushed it under water until the young man almost ceased to struggle. Letting him up and waiting for him to regain his composure, the teacher asked the student, " when you were under the water, what did you want more than anything in the world ", the student replied, " the thing I wanted more than anything, was air ". The lesson? When you want knowledge, the way that the young man desired air, that's when you will
get it.

That is what we must have, we must want it like air, we must want knowledge like air, wisdom like air, success, like air, freedom, justice, and equality, like air. That's where Black America came from, where our ancestors came from, that is how our forefathers and predecessors endured hard trials and overcame tremendous, almost insurmountable obstacles to give us, their descendants and beneficiaries, the very opportunity that we have to be alive today.

Much of the world does look to America as the light of leadership, for untold millions it represents hope, that which gives life and expression to the very idea of freedom. And a vast majority of the world of color, the Afro-Asiatic world that includes the greater proportion of the more than six billion souls on earth, looks to

Black America. They know our history, have watched us during our journey, and most, especially in the so-called third world, identify their struggle, with our struggle.

Even in this new era of time, too many millions of African-Americans look at themselves and allow themselves to be defined, publicly and privately, by a false history that began and ends with slavery, perpetuating self hate, defeat and no self esteem.

Search the Internet, study world literature and history, understand our real and ancient connections with the human family and the roles our ancestors have played, then we will perhaps, appreciate the high expectations they may have of their millions of African-American brothers and sisters.

The descendants of west Africa's Moorish empires have a rich and glorious history and a wealth of philosophic, esoteric, spiritual, and mystical traditions. Higher learning and the sciences that had been used to build and maintain the world's great civilizations, from ancient Khamet (Egypt), to Arabia, Persian, pre and post Aryan India, to renaissance Europe, Great Britain and the United States of America.

Do African Americans owe it to themselves and especially, with emphasis, owe it to their children, to re-acquire the knowledge, wisdom, and understanding of their ancestors. By what ever true and useful means available, to reacquire our heritage and birthrights, even from those who have " adopted " the light of our ancestors as their own and for their own purposes and use, those very impregnable doctrines that would empower us to take our rightful places in the affairs of men.

Countless millions of our brothers and sisters have walked away from knowledge, have turned their backs on understand and determined, that any education the mythological "white man" has, is not worth having, not realizing that most of the true knowledge in America, even what is used as the foundational operating principles of this great nation, is knowledge gleaned from the sacred sciences of our own ancestors.

Understandably, most if not all institutions of learning in the United States, were basically established and are presently controlled by Caucasian people and are designed according to their history, traditions, and worldview, which is why, most if not all of the history taught in the U.S., is more European history or within the borders of this country,"White" American history, with Black history as something of an afterthought.

That is one of the difficult challenges that confront us, we must master two schools of thought, two ways of life, one Eurocentric and the other Afrocentric.

This is in no way suggesting  it to be meant that
anyone must " be white ", that is an impossibility, but
to be knowledgeable enough of truth to function
effectively, for one to grow and prosper, to reach any
and all the heights possible in America.

What is there on the bottom? We have been on the
bottom and been there long enough,the only way left
to go is up!


There are instances where far too much is made of
names or designations and titles, confusion is the usual
outcome as the vitally important discussions are lost in
issues of semantics, the meanings of words and
phrases.
A majority of African-American people have already
abandoned the names of negro, black, and colored, and
we thank God, that we're certainly come a long way
from when we were ALL flat out called niggers!

That name may never be banned from use until every
African American out lives and lives above its most
negative and historical connotations.

It is imperative that we all regain our global
consciousness, each one of our children must be taught

to think, act, and live as part of the global community. We must by absolute necessity so construct our lives, that they be the exact opposite of of the mischaracterizations, stereotypes, and misconceptions that some disillusioned members of the larger society insist on subjecting us to, based on nothing more than their vain imaginations and darkest fears, they are the dedicated enemies against our restoration.

Could the world-wide impact be imagined, should millions of Africa's most precious descendants, that carry within them, the DNA of the greatest builders of civilizations the world has ever seen, that they should realize their vast potential, realize who they really are, and who their forefathers were, moreover, to assume their spiritual and intellectual statue.

This was, and remains, the revolutionary idea, the completely different paradigm.

There are a number of organizations, that have worked to help African American people in the transformational process, and, since the beginning of the 1900s, groups such as the United Negro improvement association of the honorable Marcus Garvey, the Niagara movement, some of the Black churches, and other traditional religious organizations, the Black Masonic lodges and fraternities, along with a collection of smaller eastern Islamic groups that have made meaningful contributions.

A picture may in fact say more than a thousand words, just look at the pictures from around the world, look at people from around the entire globe, from every walk of life, and how they respond to America's first " Black " president, ( in 300 years at least) , look at how their children respond, and that should tell you that the world knows who you are and who your forefathers were. The world knows what Black America is capable of, they are waiting for us to wake up and act like we know.

There are countless individuals, that, without their significant contributions, there could not have been any progress, and their many notable and outstanding achievements are undeniable, we should all recognize and respect them.

A major reason for the problems that we are having with our young people, is because we have withheld from them the " naked truth " about our American experience, and, the liberating truth, that they are not the images, stereotypes, or historical representations of dumb, inferior, failure-characterizations, used to keep them psychologically defeated. Subsequently, they are confused, and unable to find their places in the scheme of things.

In the forefront of the struggle at the turn of the
century, was Noble Drew Ali's Moorish Science
Temple of America. Which by 1925, was firmly
established in over 15 different states, and
headquartered in Chicago Illinois. In the midst of "The
Great Black Migration", as millions traveled north,
seeking better economic conditions, all of these
different organizations and groups were laboring to
better the overall conditions of Black people in
America, not quite 50 years after emancipation and the
release from physical slavery.

Drew Ali's movement, which would go on to become
the first and largest mass Islamic organization in
American history, presented Black America with a
viable answer, a workable solution to what was called
at that time "The Negro Problem" or "the American
Dilemma".

If we are ever to take our rightful places in the affairs
of this country, if America is to ever live out the
true meaning of her creed, then this we must
understand, even from the very foundations of this
country, there have always been unique, distinguished
types of citizens, who believed in a type of freedom, a
level of civilization, most Americans have yet to fully
appreciate.

The American idea has yet to be fully unfolded into

reality for all of her people, this has not been lost on
the men and women who, throughout our history, have
given everything, including their lives, to make
freedom a reality. It has been a long and difficult
process, and there are even greater challenges in front
of us.

We must reassess our values, renew our commitments,
and reconsider our purposes . It is in fact, one of the
most important individual responsibilities, that we are
knowledgeable and informed enough
to be valuable assets to our country, our communities,
our families and friends. That we position ourselves
to always be part of finding and implementing
solutions rather than to be found among those who
always manage to create more problems than they
solve.

Despite the effects of the twisted history, the distorted
stereotypes, and the misconceptions, myths, and
outright lies, that have been a part of traditional
American lore, or the undeniable, debilitating,
devastating effects that have historically impeded the
forward progress of African American people, a
truthful and accurate account of our history, the
knowledge of ourselves, our divine rights, and
privileges, and with the help of divine providence,
there is every necessary resource available, beginning
with the work of Drew Ali, to raise the self-image and

the collective consciousness of Black-America, for the first time in ages, above ground level.

The foundation stone has been set in the true knowledge of self, and every excuse has been taken away.
We shall be forever in the debt of those who have sacrificed beyond our estimation and are even now working to recover our " stolen legacy ", perhaps much to the chagrin of those who lightly dismiss and lament 'ad infinitum' that Prophet Drew Ali " borrowed " from Masonic and other sources " in constructing his movement and temple, also in formulating his sacred doctrine.

When asked how he was going to wake up the sleeping Moors, ( teach the so-called Negro, Black, Colored, etc. about the glorious knowledge of themselves, who their ancient forefathers were, and how they could rise and overcome the dark legacy of slavery ), the Holy Prophet said he was going to
*" wake them up in love "*.

There are many great and noble Moorish leaders in America today, adepts, officials, and others in authority who claim their mission and light to be that of the great Prophet of Ali, but like others they also have " slouched under the wings of their cross to extract from those that come to them that means

whereby they may enjoy the pleasures of this life ",
rather than aid in the great work of uplifting their own
people, to teach them the things necessary to become
better citizens, and to be willing to love instead of to
hate.

" We may believe what others say, but in that manner
never truly know...if man would know, he must himself be what he knows ".  This highlights the absolute
necessity for each individual's investment in personal
enrichment and preparation, by study, research, the
most diligent inquiry, honest living, and unfeigned
sincerity.

It is troubling and disingenuous for those who insist on
spreading hatred and divisiveness in the name of
Moorish Science, and teaching things that are clearly
the exact opposite of what the American Prophet
Noble Drew Ali taught, teaching the very opposite of
his' philosophy, whether social, moral, or spiritual, as
we have it recorded in various literature that can be
directly attributed to the organization and movement
that he founded.

If we would just choose instead to speak and live
positively, we would see things in a very different
light. There's a powerful, overlooked, connection
there, between speaking and thinking. We cannot see
the light, walk in the light or be the light, if we insist

on speaking and living in the ways of Darkness.

Perhaps this is the very reason that Ali believed that we needed more than anything, to " learn to love instead of to hate ".

Of what benefit is it to speak despairingly of others, how can we determine the hearts of people that we have never met, this is foolishness, and the wise man leaves no time for foolishness.

For obvious reasons, much is made of the Moorish Temple's masonic appearance, the popular speculation is for the most part erroneous, and the public distortions, slandering, injurious comments made by a few wrong-spirited Moorish "Grand Sheiks" and "adepts", has only added more confusion to an already hotly debated, contentious, divisive issue.

One should really take a glance at the various requirements of the 32 degrees which make up the masonic super structure, read some of the books that described its history, philosophy, aims, and purpose. Talk to some of its members, before deciding to publicly slander thousands, if not, millions of people, based on personal bias and insufficient knowledge. We should be mature enough to admit to ourselves that we cannot possibly know everything about every one, neither should we ever put everyone into the same category or judge everyone in that manner.

For any person to master the entire masonic system of esoteric and symbolic instruction and training, is no small accomplishment, and definitely requires self-discipline and a highly developed intellect. Nevertheless, it is not the end all of spiritual, meta-physical awareness, growth, or progress.

Though there exists very little material public ally available,that would settle the issue as to whether Noble Drew Ali had accomplished the first through the thirty-second degrees, crossed to the mystic shrine, received advanced instructions, initiations and training in Morocco, Egypt, and Mecca. The picture of Sultan Abdul Abu Aziz Saud, which appears in every official publication of the "Moorish circle-seven Koran" seems to be presented as tacit approval of that possibility.

Certainly unlikely to be without dispute, such a scenario could assist in interpreting the succession of events in the life and works of the illustrious Prophet and present a more universally applicable context in which his social, philosophical, or esoteric concepts may be studied and appreciated.

There is indisputable evidence that the work of the Noble Drew Ali has been overwhelmingly successful in some respects, especially as it concerns the dissemination of knowledge, of the secret history of America, her African descendants, and the diffusion of "masonic-type" knowledge, eastern mysticism, as well as oriental philosophy throughout the psychic life-stream of Black America.

*"The object of our organization is to help in the great work of uplifting fallen humanity and to teach those things necessary to make better citizens of men and women."*

The actual underpinnings of America's free-national form of citizenship and government are little understood or known by most Americans in general, and African Americans in particular.

Used in different fraternal, occult, mystical, masonic-type philosophical groups, several of their doctrines define " the Great Work " in similar language, usually with ultimate reference to the entire body of humanity's spiritual restoration, to a plane of life and intelligence, unknown since the proverbial "fall of man". Neither have accomplishments in man's spiritual growth or other notable work been confined to any one particular group, despite many fantastic claims.

This, in the final analysis, may serve as a designated mission statement, in our humble attempt to ascertain the Prophet's intended trajectory for his' " Divine and National Movement. Drew Ali's racial concepts, have been troubling for many, especially the way in which he defines 'black', as according to science meaning,"death". However, that definition is taken from what becomes Ali's esoteric teachings, which must be viewed in conjunction with his approach to solving the "Negro problem", or separating traditionally "Black" people from the oppressive racial distinctions that were conceived and used historically in American law and public to effectively bar our people from access to the full statue of American citizenship and privileges.

Perhaps he was attempting to define Black-America's unique position, as outside the true Constitutional parameters, isolated from the human family in general and the constitutional family of free-national citizens out of every country around the world in particular, i.e. all free American citizens, recognized as German-American, Chinese-American, Italian-American, Iraqi-American, Mexican-American etc., while the descendents of Africa are still, in the twenty-first century, treated and classified by bogus racial classifications.

While appealing to "the Negro", to realize that he was in a fallen condition ( not without also having been pushed ), "in sin", by not being more intelligent

59

leaders, committed citizens and family men, "industrious" people as their forefathers had been for thousands of years. Ali taught that all people have suffered in the bondage of slavery and that we also suffered slavery, as a result of our turning to sin and turning away from the true God.

The greater the number of everyday people, that come to realize who they are and the untapped potential that is available to enable them to better their conditions, the more clearly they will understand and appreciate what the world expects from us and why.

The Moors were instructed to honor Jesus, Buddha, Confucius, and Mohammed, to honor all true and divine Prophets, to study and practically apply the teachings. Ali's manner of life, from what can be determined, shows a man at ease on every plane of life, also one able to interact ,communicate, and work with men and women from vastly different areas of life.

For a so-called "man of color" in 1911 America, when most people were still using horses and wagons, Noble Drew Ali had a very wide appeal and extensive media coverage in many areas of the country. That, including the first mass Islamic type movement or organization developed among African American people in the history of the country.

All indications are that Drew Ali, above all others, believed in the final restoration and salvation of his people through re-education, nationalization, and spiritual re-birth. The Egyptian Adept successfully combined all the necessary and divergent elements of knowledge, information and divine wisdom, into a philosophical synthesis that was designed to accomplish that end.

For the overwhelming majority of African- Americans at that time, their knowledge of race, history, and interactions between different countries and nations of the world was mostly limited to the isolated American media, adjusted to public opinion, for public consumption, and their own history lost in the black mists of slavery, most Blacks were effectively kept in a state of suppressing ignorance and subservience.

Those are the very reasons that we must abandon those names and their definitions that serve only to constantly resurrect and perpetuate the psychologically debilitating, inhibiting, depressive and socially crippling mentality among African-Americans and our children, ensuring a life of defeat, hatred and self-doubt.
The " American Dilemma" is being solved only as it can be, through the process of time, change, and intellectual as well as spiritual growth, reconfiguring public awareness with the knowledge of the truth.

61

## Chapter Three:  In an Intelligent Tone

*"Like unto trees of gold arranged in beds of silver are wise sentences uttered in due season."*

In today's world, of things deemed vitally important, effective communication  is critical, a workable knowledge and effective use of language is essential, and for the contemplation of spiritual realities, a refined intelligence is indispensable.

What discloses the level of insight that we have genuinely attained more accurately than our choice of words or the tone of our conversations.  We are often argumentative, when we should be consolatory, loud and abrasive, when soft-spoken and reasonable would be more effective.

The cultivating of the mind with wisdom, useful knowledge, and understanding concerning the correct principals of application, enhances the continuance and enriches the all of life.

Philosophy is the contemplative study of nature, of human knowledge, and human values, but that is not a complete or contemporary definition.  In modern usage, philosophy is a pursuit of personal knowledge, wisdom, and understanding.

It is the capacity to think clearly, reason, and perceive, beyond that which is normally considered, the contemplation of ideas of infinite concern.

Philosophy bridges the gaps between religion, spirituality, knowledge and insight gleaned from practical experience, the extra-reality of the divine, and the everyday world.

This is not to sanction the teachings of a particular 'philosopher' or their works, but to place emphasis on the practice of abstract thinking.

One's personal philosophy or proven knowledge, having been gleaned from lessons in the school of life, external concepts, religious and secular ideas, beliefs, or popular philosophies may be accepted and assimilated into one's internal frame of reference. Thus, it is an individual as well as a collective way of thinking or approach to understanding and living life.

We have our personal views, our vantage points, our way in which we see ourselves and the world around us, this is based on our collective experiences and how much accurate information we have effectively processed. This body of knowledge is our frame of reference with which we compare new information,

63

experiences, or concepts, and from which is developed our personal philosophies concerning different aspects of life.  Let us here coin a phrase, " we should never measure another person's intelligence by our own, we will usually give ourselves too much credit ".
Different groups, communities, states, and nations develop a type of collective consciousness, which may be called " public opinion " or " general opinion ", neither of which are at any time necessarily true, but normally influences, if not determines the approved laws, customs, or traditions. Public opinion is affected by the amount and quality of knowledge available in the public sector, regarding a given
issue with which the population must be concerned.

Compounding the challenge, is that, we must master two entirely different bodies of knowledge and diametrically opposite ways of life, which, to our benefit, may be a blessing in disguise. We must know and master ourselves and our own culture and knowledge, in addition, we must master to a certain extent, American culture and knowledge to have increased opportunities to be successful Americans. Because in the final analysis, that level of investment in the acquisition of all useful knowledge, wisdom, and understanding, has become absolute requirements for ourselves, our children, and our children to come.

Understanding this, that the only way out of our

vicious cycle, the only way Black America will finally overcome, is to over come. We have never been given any other option, there will be no violent revolution, the only way out, really is *up*.

The Moorish-American nationality and religious template will not work for every Black American, however, it has provided a means whereby the descendants of Africans in American, can choose to redefine themselves, develop their own unique cultural identity, religious preferences, history, past and present day world-view, independent of the biased, bogus, uniquely American system of racial classification.

Even if American by actual birth, non-Europeans are still automatically relegated to positions of self perpetuating inferiority, due to the continued use of the exact same system of social order that has been used and enforced since slavery began in this country.

*" You who doubt whether I, the Prophet, and my principals are right for the redemption of my people, go to those that know law, in the City Hall and among the officials in your government and ask them under an intelligent tone, and they will be glad to render you a favorable reply, for they are glad to see me bring you out of darkness into light. "*     Drew Ali

The historical emancipation of millions of slaves in one fell swoop, originally exacerbated the problem. With little more than literally the clothes on their backs, most of the now former slaves could not afford to even move away from the plantations, most continue to work for food, clothing, and a shack to live in. Then was born the sharecropping system, practically a revised and updated form of indentured servitude (working for credit), a system that has worked so well, that it has continued with a few modifications since that time.

The legal proposals, that had called for reparations to the new citizens of 40 acres and a mule as compensation for their generations of injury and damages, as well as the means to establish themselves with homesteads, farmland, and other opportunities, were quietly removed from the table of American jurisprudence. Later, the 14th and 15th amendments were enacted in a feeble attempt to repair what was quickly becoming "a tumor on the body of the state". Some constitutional privileges were granted that assimilated the ex-slaves into the body politic without any remedy or prima facie evidence of due process.

Thus were untold millions of psychologically destroyed men, women, and children cast onto the

American landscape, forced to begin their quest for freedom, justice, and the opportunity to merely engage in the pursuit of happiness, being almost 300 years behind the progress of the entire population!


Let us consider then, the social climate for Black America at the beginning of the 1900s, a period not quite 50 years, from legally sanctioned enslavement, even then Black America remained disproportionately at the bottom of the bottom, of the lowest economic and social class. Into this scenario stepped the different black spiritual, intellectual, social, and national leaders, to take on the Herculean task of uplifting their people.

Around 1911 ad., In Newark, New Jersey, Timothy Drew, to be known as Noble Drew Ali, established the first of his Moorish Science Temples ( originally the Holy Canaanite temple ), for what he proclaimed was the " great work " of uplifting fallen humanity. Ali, was the first to introduce the idea of using the Islamic creed of the east, " adapted as far as possible to Americanize life ", as a vehicle of spiritual redemption for Black Americans and he established a federally recognized, lawfully chartered organization to achieve that end. In addition, Drew Ali taught his people that they could reinstate themselves into the family of nations by abandoning the slave classifications of

67

negro, black, and colored, then recovering and proclaiming their historic, spiritual, biological, and cultural connections, through the last political and religious empire in Africa, the Moorish kingdom of northwest.

The true definitions of Constitutional American freedom and citizenship had been buried beneath the rubble of public opinion and massive ignorance on the part of the general population. The United States was literally constructed by men who were philosophers, mystics, idealist, free thinkers and free-masons, men who incorporated their visions of a people and government that lived according to the true science of life, this is why America has been called "The Great Experiment".

Though citizenship was open to all free-national beings, slaves by virtue of them being considered property, went down on the constitutional record as three fifths of being human, lacking demonstrative knowledge of ancestral descent, and spiritual heritage.

This set the stage for millions of Black people to be born in complete darkness and ignorance concerning knowledge of the true nature of life, of themselves or their glorious history, confused, by the religion of their oppressors and the brutal conditions that they were forced to live under, by what they were told was the will of that God.

Now several centuries later some of the descendents of those people have recovered their forefathers vast estates, have overcome the colonial seals and achieved great things, while others have languished in the names, principals, and lifestyles of spiritual darkness, completely devoid of the sacred knowledge common to some extent among all knowledgeable and informed people.

For such reasons, Drew Ali' teachings stressed a return, not merely to an original religion, but to the fundamental ideas, the very essence of religion. The Moorish scientist worked to supplant the names and contorted views of African-Americans, who were for the most part, in a wild Diaspora outside the permitted bounds of "the Great Society ". The Prophet's work was to uplift his fallen and downtrodden people, by the restoration of an accurate, positive self-image, and world-view.

It is difficult in these present times, for us to really visualize such great national movements among African-American people, with millions of Blacks who sympathized and often donated to them financially, even if they were not members.

The Moorish  Movement at it's peak would influence untold numbers of people, revive neighborhoods,

69

establish businesses and generate a substantially large amount of revenue for any religious organization at that time.

Though the movement subsided at the death of it's founder, many of the Noble Prophet's "adepts" afterwards spread across the country and to other countries, some going  underground , others starting mystical, religious, or Moorish temples and orders of their own.

Ali's original spirit and doctrine  has had an immeasurable influence on the several national Moorish Science Temples that have survived, as well as some African-American Islamic organizations, esoteric bodies and a host of different black leaders.

We can overcome, if we can understand things clearly and in the context of the times in which they happened. Looking beyond the turbulent history of these United States, we can see the context in which our true history had such a profound effect on our American experience, and why. We must come to understand these things intelligently and un-emotionally.

We must understand that the "American" definitions and classifications of people, emerged as the country grew and the economy grew, as the means of

70

controlling growth, development and power, and to justify the inhuman treatment and exploitation of Africans. We should consider these things when we determine what we are, who we are, and perhaps most important, what we can accomplish. Can we accept the fact, that the world will never be convinced of our genuine determination, nor willing to contribute to our restoration, by what we say, but by what we accomplish.

It is a settled historical fact, that our direct African ancestors raided the coasts of Europe, pillaging, killing, and taking Europeans captive into slavery for hundreds, if not thousands of years.

Of course the business of slaves was practiced all over the world but no where was it to take on the brutality and inhumanity as in America, where millions of human beings were unceremoniously stripped of their individual human rights, freedom, self-worth, nationalities or ethnic identities, history, religion, even language, and demoted by law and public practice to a status equal with horses, cattle or other livestock.

In the " brave new world ", the whole concept of "identity", was twisted grotesquely, into a psychological abnormality.
With America's geographical isolation from the rest of the world, it allowed the preferences of racial

71

superiority doctrines that surfaced along with the theories of "survival of the fittest " and "evolution", to subject Blacks to the most vicious system of dehumanization and oppression that the world had ever seen.

But that is history, and in these days there is a much different, more potentially devastating form of slavery, and that is mental slavery, spiritual darkness, living outside the bounds of righteousness as outcast, criminals, outlaws, and " undesirables ".

There is a way forward for "Black America", there is in fact but one way, and that is by sheer determination. With the spiritual enlightenment of the unenlightened, educating, preparing and qualifying ourselves, and the multitudes of our precious young men and young women who are presently being disposed of in record numbers. They can and they must be tomorrow's innovators, entrepreneurs, adventurers, business magnates, educators and world changers.

In this 21st century, with an exploding population and dwindling resources, we can expect the struggle to survive and the competition for those resource to become much more intense. In American, where information and life is quite literally moving faster than the speed of sound, and the cost of living is increasing at an ever quickening pace, the most important form of capital being discussed or put to use is intellectual capital. We are by no means living in a post racial America, but we have reached a point as a nation, as a modern society, and as one of the most advanced nations on earth where intellectual capital, where useful knowledge, knowledge that is in demand can not afford to discriminate quite as much.

" This is a new era of time ", a global society and world community, in which the African American community, along with all the other nations and ethnic groups on earth, must engage in "mutual helps and reciprocal obligations", to facilitate the continued growth and development of the human family.
We know that we need all of the best and the brightest, and of course, a " mind is a terrible thing to waste ".

## Chapter Four: The Lessons of Love Divine

That faith, resident, in the sacred doctrine of Ali's
Moorish Science, is in essence the same as in all true
and divine religions, that holy faith, in which all men
of truth can find agreement.

In the zealous doctrine of Mohammed, the absolute
God sent extreme laws for extreme conditions,
Buddha's lessons met the need for universal
compassion, Confucius taught men to think, and then
to think again, the Christ brought the kingdom of
heaven and victory over death.

In taking a conscious step into the world of things
made manifest, one must decisively choose the way of
love instead of hate, if there be any hope of fulfilling
the true purpose of life. How many have tried the life
of darkness and been themselves destroyed and
brought to ruin by the hatred and isolation it brings.

By the initial processes of our nature we learn to be
attached, in love with physical things and the physical
world, we lose the consciousness thereby, of the Holy
One, of His love and his peace. The noble decision to
be a builder rather than a destroyer, which the words

adept, philosopher or mason actually imply, those will become proficient in the understanding and the application of the lessons taught through the various traditional, ancient and contemporary avenues of philosophical, mystical, or spiritual learning.

To posse the knowledge of the truth, to aid our brother man, to be of use to or country and nation, to uplift ourselves and take every opportunity to participate in the uplifting of others, to know our God and submit to His will for our lives, such is the duty of man.

But carnal men never want the light; they *" love the dark, because their deeds are evil.."*

Every true and divine prophet must contend with the initial rejection and harsh treatment, their messages are almost always universally rejected at first and never the message that the people desire to hear.

Fleshly minded men love the empty forms, the pomp and circumstance, pageantry and the extravagance of eye pleasing ceremonies, all the glamor of pretension after which there is nothing more required.

To overcome a predominantly European centered theological super-structure, in which God was "white" and his people were "black", quite at a disadvantage psychologically to start, Drew Ali selected an all encompassing religious ideology.

Practitioners of Moorish Science work to " honor " (study, respect, teach) all true and divine prophets, Jesus, Buddha, Confucius, and Mohammed, with the addition of 18 years of Jesus' life used as an esoteric template, illustrated by various symbols and mystical accounts of the life works, teachings and ministry of the Christ.

The Prophet Noble Drew Ali's doctrine of Islamism is presented in cryptic, unconventional language, as an abstract synthesis of religious faith, philosophical knowledge, and mystical illumination.

Even today, some are confused by what is thought to be Ali's racial definitions, of black, which he defined as " according to science means death, and "white", which his literature says " means purity, purity means god, and god means the ruler of the land ".

To avoid the confusion which will quite naturally happened, it must be remembered that Moorish Science teaches that there can in reality be no such thing as " colored people ", black or white.  The answer is found in the temple's teachings from their Holy Koran, pertaining to the death, burial, and resurrection of the Christ, and his sacred connection with the "silent brotherhood", among whom white was symbolic of purity and light.

Our inner life, our thoughts, feelings, emotions, communications with our fellow men, should cause us to ask ourselves some hard questions, questions that we may have avoided asking in the past.

What would happen if we changed our ways of thinking, our views of life in general and life in America in particular? What would happen if we continue to rediscover and redefine ourselves? What if we just flat out refuse to continue being victims? What if we choose to believe, despite any disagreement, that we can be the best instead of the worst? What if we choose to allow our true history, the wisdom, knowledge and understanding of the sacred sciences of our forefathers to reignite hope?

What would happen in our communities, temples, churches and schools, if they refused to participate in the perpetuation of the distorted and untrue versions of history, but rather with due diligence, wrote our own history? Simply refuse to participate, do our own research, adhere to our own worldview.

The observant see an ever living, all powerful- God, in their lives and in the lives of others, even in the

multifarious experiences of seemingly mundane life.
Religion should help us in our noble pursuits of truth,
philosophy should assist us in thinking intensely and
profoundly, sincerity should encourage us to continue
in what is right.

Is there any phenomena more interesting, thought
provoking or at times humorous, as those few, the self
defined "true believers", to the usual exclusion of all
others. The special few, who take upon themselves
the task of correcting everyone else, demanding that
all must conform to their ideas of what is correct and
fit into some particular box.

In view of these things we have this to say, of all
knowledge, self knowledge is important, but God
knowledge is vitally important.

One without knowledge of self is like a tree without
roots, one without knowledge of God has yet to
become a tree.
We discover that even anger is good energy, which,
when harnessed and focused by the power of a
concentrated thought, is effective fuel, a motivating
power, capable of energizing us, enabling us to
perform the most difficult task or endure the most
strenuous circumstances, in order to reach our desired
goals.

Some elements and practices of modern business have had, perhaps unintended, but nevertheless devastating effects on the mental health and self esteem of the general population. Teaching people through the effects of their advertising, to be ashamed of or to hate different things about themselves, pointing out unacceptable deficiencies of appearance, size, material possessions or the lack thereof, as things they suggest are imperfections and therefore must be changed.

One must not submit to nor be overcome by public perception, forced by mere peer pressure to conform to an idea that is untenable (cannot be defended), as well as belittling, disgusting, and derogatory.

To take one's place in the world, one must of necessity be determined to act according to law, only those that abide within the law ( law-abiding citizens ), can demand equal protection and application of lawful directives to the body (the people and government), which are regulated by the " law of the land ", and to which the law gives life. All others ie. criminals, aliens, undesirables, etc., exist outside the sheltering parameters of the law ( outlaws ), are classified and treated as enemies of the peace, and retain the barest rights under this Constitution.

Then there is that which life demands, and the watchful presence of Omniscience ensures that all comply with the internal and external, unalterable laws of the universe.

It is in the heart of a living soul, that true altar fires of love divine are set ablaze with love of God and all of life. No infinite God would be entertained by our piteous posturing, where can be found such an omniscient One who would trouble Himself to give ear to the counsel of men?

In our initial, embryonic states of developing cognizance of life, light and truth, we can make very little sense of things, which are at first obscure, and the fundamental instructions are always seemingly imperfectly explained. The less patient, disobedient, and rebellious are certain to race.." without complete if any knowledge of where they are going or what their end will be".

We gain proficiency through the understanding and application of the various lessons that are taught through the mediums of spiritual text , philosophical and esoteric literature, traditions, symbolism and the affairs of life, ordered and directed by Divine Wisdom.

Over time, bits of information, flashes of insight or intuition, concerning the 'chokma nistra', or "hidden wisdom, are acquired and accumulated, knowledge that for considerable periods of time may appear, in some instances, is, in opposition. Perseverance, coupled with the utmost sincerity, brings clarity and the additional ability to perceive, to distinguish light from darkness, truth from error, building blocks from useless rubble.

The master-workman wields the hammer of the will, "driving in the truth," until it is a part of every part, the inner temple rises squarely on the solid foundation of practical experience.

The practice of religion for such a one becomes a living faith, "..one great drama for the sons of men", a man made strong (spiritually) in life, and light " by buffeting and woes of many kind ".

Religion, like the Sabbath, was made to serve man, man was not made to serve religion. True religion, is a means to an end, a journey, way of living, it is a process not an event. It is not for outward show, but for inner peace, neither should it be used as a way of impressing others, but the growth, development, empowering of the real man, the better man, the higher-self.

Some mature by this means, others by another, a few, seem never to grow at all, therefore are we encouraged to keep our passions and desires within the bounds of moderation, refusing to entertain those thoughts, that we have learned by experience, have the tendency and power to divert us from the righteous path.

Through the life of the Christ is taught all the lessons of purity and love, and the supreme lesson, "the manifest of love, raised from the dead".

"Your Holy Bible", records the public life and teachings of Jesus, his parables and prophecy, also his trial, death and resurrection from the dead. The "18 missing years", are the esoteric focus of the Moorish Koran, or "the circle seven's lessons". Ali may have use the coded language of these teachings to communicate the secrets of those pristine doctrines to his followers.

However, Drew Ali was not the first to publish accounts of a secret life of Christ, accounts "from the East" have appeared in western religious thought periodically for centuries. In the 1890s, Nicholas Notovich, a Russian journalist, published a book about the unknown life of Jesus which mentions Tibetan records located at a Buddhist monastery, which also offer details of Jesus' travels in India.

There are religious records in Indian temples that record the work of a Yesu, born miraculously, proclaimed a savior, and taught a virtuous doctrine, ancient Persian historical documents also mentions a

Jesus.

Many of these works from eastern sources found their way to the west, were translated into different languages, in different countries, some in which it was acknowledged what their sources were, in others, publishers claimed some type of revelation or as their own original work.

In 1908, the Aquariun gospel of Jesus the Christ was published by one Levi Dowling, a former Christian Sunday school teacher and Baptist minister, and from all accounts a researcher into the divine sciences or the ancient wisdom.

Levi claims to have read the Akashic records and received communications directly from celestial angels, all experiences which culminates into his book.

The Dead Sea scrolls, discovered in a cave near the Dead Sea, the sight of a monastic brotherhood, who in their literature identify themselves with "the sons of light", a spiritual, mystical brotherhood, very much like the "silent brotherhood", that Drew Ali makes use of and thought by some of today's writers to be where both John the Baptist and Jesus received their initial preparations, teachings and training for their public ministries.

83

The above information, and much more besides, has been known but suppressed by official Church bodies and other ecclesiastical authorities, that they could concentrate on furthering their own peculiar agendas. This may be what Drew Ali meant by "the first church, that crucified Jesus for seeking to redeem his' people..", the Church at Rome was assimilated into the body of the State, became an organ of the State and finally, a creation of the State.

That is the " man made religion ", specially crafted to produce a mythologized racial superiority complex that welded a national bond and sustained an iron handed rule. That may very well be the church to be returned to those who established it , not for any love of Jesus, but to manipulate and fleece the populace, influence the course of nations and rule in wealth and absolute sovereignty on the earth, perhaps that can be called "earthly salvation".

The Moorish Science instead, is a method of philosophical symbolism and parabolic instructions, the imputation of the science of the ancient wisdom, the sacred doctrine, as it ever has been, communicated by symbols, analogy, parable and metaphors.

Ali was the first to teach the " Asiatics " of America about a Jesus that, even according to their Bibles, looked like them, and descended ultimately from the same people as they did, a Jesus they could believe in.

It is very interesting that the Buddha is portrayed as a veritable "African Negro", complete with beaded hair, thick lips, and broad nose over most if not all of Asia.

# Chapter Five:  Defending the Faith

A great deal of thought, preparation and labor goes into every act of establishing a movement, a spiritual, religious, fraternal, or civic organization. In the preliminary stages of any work, trial and error are a natural part of perfecting a work and tailoring it to fit the prevailing circumstances.

It can be quite a daunting task, to locate a Moorish temple group that adheres to the original doctrine and practices of the "illustrious Prophet". Few of the Prophet's laws will lend even the slightest agreement to current practices of some  Moorish Science Temple groups, that have more in common with present day Arabic Muslims and their religious views.

Various study groups, societies, temples, orders, and at least in one instance, a church, now make use of the Noble Prophet Drew Ali's archive of mystic and divine import, to pursue with intuitive and perceptive inquiry, the great mysteries of man, of nature and of God, contemplating the processions of the spiritual luminaries.

A few have strayed far enough from the Teachings of love, truth, peace, freedom, and justice, that it is

difficult to recognize them as Moorish scientist, but
rather as disseminaters of confusion, crass sarcasm and
personal attacks on their rivals or dissenters, real or
imagined, all of which appears to consume the most of
their energies.

How so many, especially those assuming positions of
authority, power, and responsibility, have arrived at
such nefarious conclusions, concerning the aims of the
Prophet or the Temple, and of special note, the
consistent slandering of other organizations, of which
they obviously know little to nothing, is beyond even
basic comprehension.

There is a means whereby religion, becomes more
about man than about God, where behind a veneer of
piety or holy zeal, people work to further their own
social, political or other agendas, usually confined to a
select group, rather than any genuine concern for
every member of the human family.

All true and divine religions teach the Omnipotent,
Omniscient, One, true God and Father of all, but all
people do not see or approached him alike. Men name
the part of Allah that they can see, and this to them is
all of Allah, neither are they capable of appreciating or
considering the views and concepts of others.

Every divinely established religion, even the Islam of ancient Arabia, has an esoteric core empowering and perpetuating it's external order and organization. Likewise the more speculative areas of inquiry, the developing and use of human perception, reasoning, logical and intuitive powers.

Noble Drew Ali had no obvious intentions of adopting any everyday Arabic customs, neither did he wear a fez or his adept attire daily, but apparently a business suit or other suitable clothing. The Moors were a religious and political force in Chicago of the 1920s, due to a reported membership of thousands in the city alone.

The Moorish leader makes a clear distinction, when he identifies Mohammed as the founder of the Mohammedan religion, rather than the originator, founder, nor first practitioner of the way of Islam itself. The great Qur'an, the holy book of Islam as revealed to the Prophet Mohammed, teaches that Islam (submission to The will of Allah), was the faith of Abraham, and the original first man.

The Moorish-Americans demonstrated their faith at yearly conventions, through the operation of their temples, the language of their official charters, and of special interest, the grand, extravagant parades in Chicago at the Moorish conclaves, the Holy Prophet, sheiks, adepts and members, all in traditional ancient Moorish and Khametian holy garbs, complete with camels.

Such public parades, processions of the sacred articles, circumnavigations, are even in present times conducted by local masonic, shrine, elks, or other fraternal, secret society types. Though the Moorish presented a public national aspect of their organization, considering also the preceding statements, with the tacit acknowledgment of the Adept Chamber of the Moorish Science Temple of America inc. (3rd heaven) as the Temple's esoteric (masonic character if you will) aspect, and the expressive posture of the Moors, it is clear that most of the Moorish- Americans understood the Prophet and the Temple on more than a western masonic level and acted accordingly.

With the exception of the honorable Marcus Garvey's UNIA, Drew Ali's Divine and National Movement gave indirect, and in a few cases, direct birth, to several branches of orthodox and unorthodox Islamic organizations, a handful of national Moorish Science temples, numerous pseudo-masonic orders and groups, as well as made the practice of Eastern religious faiths more public ally allowed even if not easily accepted.

Noble Drew Ali published a short but insightful " plea

89

to the Nation ", wherein he states, *" I have suffered much and severely in the past through misunderstanding of what the movement was dedicated to "*. Ali emphasizes that the Moorish movement stands for the specific principles of love, truth, peace, freedom and justice, fundamental rules of operation, by which the " great work " of the Prophet's mission of " uplifting fallen humanity " was to be accomplished.

Written near the end of his religious, philosophic, and public career, the 'strange', mysterious and untimely 'death' of the Moorish-American Prophet in 1929, seems the final confirmation of just how great the misunderstandings and work of Prophet Noble Drew Ali actually was.

It was to those who did not understand the teachings of Moorish science, and were "in the streets" and treating " whites with open contempt ", that Ali chasten with a public rebuke and command to stop causing confusion and *"flashing your cards {knowledge} at Europeans, it causes confusion! "*.

Most of the American public has always had a basic idea and understanding of Masonic type organizations and were acquainted with some of the modes and methods of their operations. It would therefore come as a complete shock to the public conscience to be exposed to information in no way prepared for public consumption.

The great mysteries of the ancients, the divine sciences of all sacred traditions have ever been protected, concealed within concentric rings of ritual, and symbols, myth, mists and clouds. Even as there now stands, the silent sentinels of the desert, with their origins unexplained, built centuries, if not millennium, before Egypt itself was an organized country.

In the great temples of the Nile, the Khametian Hierophants, High priest, and Grand Initiators, admonished every initiate, to protect with his life that which was committed to his trust and, as there were students from many parts of the world at that time, to always assume the appearance, if not the religion, among the people of their native lands.

One highly skilled adept in the use of Moorish science should be 'enlightened' enough to work effectively in any society toward the greater good, a respecter of the law and customs of what ever country he happens to be in, with conscious possession of his sacred doctrine, a moral and proper balance between his public and private life.

Near to one hundred years after the coming of the American prophet, to uplift the fallen sons and daughters of Africa, here in America, by teaching them to abandon the ancient hatreds, stand up and make a difference in the world. To put away the slave thinking and think as their pre-slavery ancestors had, to be intelligent and builders of civilization. Far too many of our young brothers are backing down from the challenge, of the task of being real men, and have chosen instead to continue in the state of mind many of the confused, angry, disoriented slaves left the plantations with, afraid and angry with normal society, viciously angry and aggressive toward anyone that looks like us.

The Moorish Koran, the character builder, and a collection of esoteric keys called the questionnaire were introduced by Professor Drew to alter the habitual inferiority thinking of his people. As the teachings of mysticism suggests, the higher practical knowledge of truths concerning God, man and the universe, are attained only by intense study, deep meditation and sharpening of the intuitive faculty.

The words "divinely prepared" should, with the radiant symbol of circle and seven on the cover be evidence enough how the contents were to be received, studied, and put into practical use. Those true secrets, that have been kept by the Moslems ( submitters or obedient ones ) , of India, Egypt and Palestine, are released in the cryptic, veiled, and coded language.

The great Temple of Ali is established as deriving its authority from the great Qur'an....to propagate the "faith" of Mohammed.

The Holy Qur'an of Mecca teaches that there is one Supreme God they call Allah and that Allah has sent prophets with the divine message to ALL people, some of them known to Mohammed, others he was not aware of (40:78) and that all religions are but one (23:52)

Ali demonstrates the divine prerogative of formulating a doctrine to meet a specified set of unique circumstances and redefines an entire multitude. Introducing the novel concept that as long as you conform to the labels of others you will be viewed and treated according to their definitions and expectations.

He re-introduced for the first time in ages to the descendants of Africa in America, the Moorish paradigm, using a synthesis of traditional degrees of west African brotherhoods, Khametian and Arabic master keys to the higher planes of life, unpublished historical accounts buried in the archives and degrees of cryptic and oriental masonry, and especially the guiding Hand of his Father-God-Allah, to bring multitudes out of the darkness of gross ignorance into the marvelous light.

But according to science, there were some who did not
want the light, they preferred the darkness because
they were slaves to sin and enjoyed evil deeds. All
indications are, that the more things change, the more
they remain the same.

Men of today are still " racing into this life without
complete if any knowledge of where they're going or
what the end will be, when riches seem to be their only
pursuit, to be obtained any way and at any cost; when
selfishness, avarice, greed and lust dominate their very
being; when humanity in general is left at the mercy of
those who have no mercy in them..", it is clearly the
time to reassess our individual and collective aims and
purposes.

The consuming desire for wealth, riches, fame,
notoriety, and the pleasures of this world rule the
hearts and minds of the many that lack discretion.
They remain hazardous, formidable rocks, on the
jagged edges of which countless lives are wrecked.
Selfishness and avarice, hatred and greed, the ignoble
crew, that steers even the captain's best ships far off
their courses.

The  Prophet's members had to prove themselves
worthy morally to be intrusted with positions of
authority in the temples or in the " Grand body of

94

Adepts ", no doubt raised  by the Egyptian Adept
himself, to the level of assimilation and active use of
the ancient wisdom.

There are more than a few indications that some of the
first to join Ali's Moorish Temples were free-masons,
philosophers, mystics of various persuasions, persons
of eastern descent, and even Europeans (whites) whom
the Prophet called "Persians or Celts".

Just before and after the turn of the twentieth century
there were a proliferation of orders, degrees,
societies, animal and working men lodges. Lovers of
eastern philosophical thought, occult teachings and
mysticism, traveled  diverse paths and through
different houses of the mystery schools in search of
arcane knowledge and spiritual illumination.

Though often confused with traditional western
masonic philosophy and practice, the body of Moorish
law is a demonstrable depository as well, of the secrets
of the east, kept in the time honored traditions of
silence and circumspection since time immemorial.

In the philosophy of Nietzsche, the "superman" idea is
the "superior man", the supposed goal of an
evolutionary struggle. It has in western application
been a mis-stating, twisting of original Asiatic

concepts of spirituality, to support impossible scenarios and create favorable atmospheres for racist, supremacy ideologies.

We find however, in the sacred universal doctrine, how man has fallen from his original state, on the higher planes of life, in the finer rates of etheric realms. Here at the rate of atmosphere, man comprehends the hidden life by what is said and done, by trial, tests, and manifold temptations, is re-acclimated to the light and re-oriented to his true center, his higher generative nature.

After formulating his Moorish doctrine, Drew Ali designated it "Islamism", not only as supposed, to distinguish his demonstration, from the orthodox beliefs of the Islamic religion, but to focus emphasis on the science, on the spiritual practice and application of the faith, rather than it's dogmatic belief systems and practices.

Islamism then, is presented as an abstract synthesis of religious faith, philosophical reasoning, mystical illumination, social resurrection, and self knowledge. Perhaps he was divinely aware of what would happen, should a large enough number of people "tap into" the boundless power of mystic thought and life.

Therefore did he open wide the doors to the school of the ancient wisdom, the knowledge of our ancestors with the admonition and caveat that one first " know thyself ".

The Moorish Adept traveled from the east coast of the country to the west, just as the mystics and philosophers of antiquity, the marabouts and holy men in oriental lands today, teaching the Faith, and establishing temples. For such has been the way of all "traveling men", who have taught the sons of men throughout all known and recorded history. The masters and students of the sacred sciences travel far and wide in search of wisdom, knowledge and truth.

It can be easily document and verified that during the Dark Ages, traveling philosophers, sages, eastern mystics of varying persuasions, crisscrossed not only Africa, Asia, or further east, such was oriental tradition since time immemorial, but across the face of Europe, instructing its nobles, laying the foundations for their schools, universities, mystic orders and initiating societies.

## Chapter Six: In The Way of Peace

*"...and the way of peace they have not known..."*

Tranquility is a state that should be common to man, the absence of emotional turbulence, peaceful and serene, even nature demonstrates harmony and equilibrium. The law of peace ensures the same to every free society, the reckless violation of which, is the cause of all injury, strife, disharmony and discord.

When any segment of the population is denied access to the full enjoyment of all rights and privileges of a free national government, by intention, omission, affecting the ability of any such group to effectively interact with the larger community, whereby any lawful citizens are omitted or disregarded, and the government becomes a participant in injuries to it's own people, it then bears responsibility for correction at law and due restitution.

Human equality in a free society must mean more than equal treatment, it must include equal access, equal opportunity in preparation and qualification. To the extent that the majority are informed and insightful, to the degree that the general consensus rest in and for support of actual justice, even so the peace, progress and prosperity of that free society is assured.

In far to many instances, modern religious groups and
their adherents are directly responsible for the
continuation and perpetuation of war, factionalism,
genocide and destruction, perfect personifications of
man's inhumanity to man.  All true and divine
religions, teach reverence for the only One, the
Omniscient, Omnipotent, Ever Living, it is in our
finite approach to the infinite, our own illusions, that
we are misled.

The majority of published information, concerning
Ali's authority and mission is conjecture for the most
part. To practically resurrect, re-constitute and
reconstruct, ethically, spiritually, and psychologically,
millions of people who were severed from the human
family, bearing little semblance to a people of free
national origin, outcast and strangers in the land of
their birth, was no task to be taken lightly.

Ali demonstrates, from what can be gleaned from
available Moorish literature, to have had a clear
conception of American's Masonic foundations and
origins, it's accommodation to freedom of inquiry, the
longstanding public policy and officially chartered
accord granting recognition of operational authority.

The illustrious Noble, understood the uniquely

American concept of personal belief and practice and from all accounts, labored to make that indelible impression on the more sincere, studious and conforming of the Moorish Americans.

It is imperative that we understand the various elements and issues involved in the creation of this country, the type of government and nation that was intended, according to surviving documents, and the type of personalities motivated and involved in America's conception and formulation.

To the detriment of a significant number of American citizens , our peculiar type of public and personal freedom is not only misunderstood but misapplied and mis-appreciated as well. All cultural and national traditions that comply with Federal and state laws or statues are accepted under the Federal Constitution and in the American forum.

*"We of the Moorish Science Temple of America, like countless other American citizens, know that we must live together here in America in harmony, friendship and goodwill, whatever our race and creed may be. It is only from a purely religious standpoint....that we differ from a large number of our fellow Americans. We believe in, and foster the Moslem religion. We believe in the principles of its' teachings insofar as*

*they can be adapted to American Life.*

*We feel that the Christian religion is all right for those who prefer it. In America, religious freedom is guaranteed under the constitution."*

The Prophet consistently demonstrated his sincere belief in the capacity of his people to succeed, and in encouraging them, he further stated.." We are interested in freeing ourselves and our children, from the greatest plight, economic slavery. We believe this can be best done by encouraging, patronizing and establishing our own business enterprises and cultivating our own acres of land. We welcome into our folds men and women of our group of all sections, all trades, occupations and professions of sound mind and good character ....".

*" ...We are friends and servants of humanity we are dedicated to the purpose of elevating the moral, social, and economic status of our people. We have set about to do this through a wide and comprehensive program embodying the principles of love, truth, peace, freedom, and justice...,".*

Perhaps, the statements above may be best summarized by Ali's very words, " I am signed up to go in a certain way with the government and I must go

101

that way!".

Our interrelations, business, cultural, and ideological exchanges, are also opportunities to develop mutual respect and appreciation, and to further our understanding of the human condition.

It may serve as a higher calling to the entirety of "Black America", to each and every one of those who have a true desire, to act in what ever capacity that they may possess, to perpetuate the forward movement of the essential ideas and instrumental principles among our people and nation.

For it is an undeniable reality and absolute certainty that we cannot afford to continue to acquiesce in any measure, to the self-destructive, self defeating behavior that we have shown toward each other, or in the larger society, inflicting more devastating damage on our own people and doing more to destroy the hope of Black America ever overcoming, than any of our racial enemies ever could.

However, Drew Ali's sagacity has, in the process of time , become clearly evident in his laying of the spiritual and civil foundations on which descendents of Africa in America can freely, collectively and/or independently, reconstruct their heritage, heal their psyche, assume their inheritance.

The essence of Ali's Moorish Science can only be imparted to minds developed enough, souls pure and skilled enough in the use of those intellectual tools, to work out to the clearest perceptible degree, all the subtle implications, enigmas, and divergent philosophical thoughts.

Nevertheless, this is a new era of time, a global village, a world community....in which the African-American community must find and fill it's useful place and  purpose, provide for it's necessary resources, establish and assert it's human and divine right in the world-wide scheme of things.

To stand idly by and do nothing, to retreat from the schools and institutions of higher learning, or abandon the halls of justice in lawful appeal, to determine open and complete hostility, in disregard for the laws of the land, will only ensure that millions of Black people, especially our strong young brothers, will continue to be herded like cattle, into the jails and prisons all over the country, or fall as victim, to another viciously angry and confused Black man, who is so full of hate, that he murders another Black man and successfully throws his own life away as well.

It is written that " there is nothing new under the sun", archaeologist now reckon civilizations by the hundreds of  thousands of years.  History fades into the dark and

103

obscure mists of time, and as far back as we look we see the rise and fall of empires, the birth of nations, and unfortunately, the destruction of populations, the extinction of entire ethnic groups of people, it being demonstrated repeatedly that only the strong survive, the weak perish.

## Chapter Seven:   A Star in the East

It was the brothers of the Magian priesthood, guided by the blazing star of heaven, who traveled the ancient way until they found that place where the holy child was incarnated.  Being yet in the formative stages, still they recognized the divine idea, that light that would illuminate the the world and prepare all men for the consummation of all things.  They faithfully followed the light, directed through dangers seen and unseen, were kept from the powers of wicked men, adored the birth of the eternal Word, and carried that word to distant lands.

*"...The Hebrew prophet is the rising star of wisdom deified, he brings to us a knowledge of the secret things of Allah; and all the world will hear his words, will heed his words, and glorify his name."*

Truth is eternal, the revelation of which must by nature, exist in all the true and divine religions, and after centuries of moral decadence and decline, the spirit life of man must be purified again.

In all systems of holy instruction and training, we find records of that same and central star of radiant elucidation, conferring divine wisdom and knowledge, revealing to man his latent potentials.

105

It is a star symbolic of man, the spirit man, that true man, the higher-self, which, with the absolute mastery and control of the lower nature, the fix, has been solved.

"Men need a pattern for their lives", in the far east, it is Buddha, while Christ is the pattern for the west, across the vast desert lands Mohammed is the model one and the meditative philosophical scholars yet walk in lands of the rising suns.

All wise men continue to follow that Star, recompensed with that mystic light of illumination, revelation, initiation and divine guidance.

Irrespective of popular perception, initiation is not a vile word, neither is it an event but rather a process of controlled growth and spiritual development, and the unveiling or revealing of that which had been previously unknown.

Whatsoever precious stones or gems the Father has vouchsafed into our care, is in truth that with which we have proven ourselves most capable of correctly perceiving, assimilating for potential and proper use and preserving from corruption or contamination.

And thus it is true on every plane of life, and those arcane processes by which the vital knowledge is acquired, by practical experience, intuitive insight and divine illumination, man by measure becomes that which he knows. Every aspirant is therefore by a progressive means in the process of becoming, this is the meaning of all the initiation and training in the transcendental disciplines.

According to the universal scheme of things, no man of flesh can raise another into consciousness of the infinite. By divine insight, wisdom and prudence, there are those that help to create environments and atmospheres that are conducive to spiritual growth, maturity and development of the latent powers of the soul. Yet it is Allah alone that can "raise thee from thou knowest not what ", into the presence of that thou knowest not what again.

One is made a son of light, a traveler on the mystic path of light and illumination, by such rites of passage and nature, will obligations ever afforded a brother or sister, every child of the true light. Their true devotion is manifested not by religious acts of piety, but in actual charity, benevolence and fellowship.

Neither is there perfect agreement among men in matters that pertain to religion, philosophy, political commentary or other issues of the day, because we are every one unique and therefore differ in some respect.

In those ancient mysteries, and especially those derived from the Khametian schools of instruction, each distinct area of life was presented as a problem to be solved, the solutions to which constituted the initiation process, with every step or degree, and, as the problems were solved, the overall quest was expanded.

The ancient "Egyptians", as they are called, developed the art of surveying the land and determining its topographical measurements, likewise did they chart the heavens and the multitude of stars, the same they did also with the life, soul and body of man.

The great pyramids were so accurately aligned and set to the cardinal points of the earth and the stars in Orion, that even in this day, they vary but slightly more than one 10th of a degree.

The greatest secrets kept inviolate in those chambers of light, were never revealed but to a handful of the highest initiates, officials, and master adepts of their sacred sciences.

The eyes of He who knows the secrets of every heart, knows those that work in sincerity, and guides such in all the ways of life, but the insincere, the workers of darkness are continually misled, confused, deceived by the very mists of darkness that envelops them.

Drew Ali proscribed a completely revolutionary paradigm for the Black Man of America to become also a resurrected son of life and light. Many of those early members were of a class that had already "traveled east in search of light", and found in the Illustrious Prophet's circle seven, an oasis in the spiritual desert of North America.

They appropriated the Moorish fez in record numbers, though in use by various western orders and native to that land where it is from it's origins crafted, it held a memorial, heartfelt, beyond the symbolic meaning for the Moorish Americans, they were in all actually returning, for the first time in ages, to a free mind, the mind of their fore-fathers.

The science of the Moors proved to be a productive confluence of Khametian mysticism, oriental philosophy and esoteric ideologies, all of which was to be comprehended by what the Moors called, the gnosis of the aught and the naught, of falsehood and of truth.

Learning to so employ the divine faculties of the higher-self, through the instruction in the ancient wisdom, by diligent study, practical application and the suffering of prudence through a proper knowledge of law.

Once capable of clearly distinguishing between the worst and best parts of our being, it is of the greatest benefit to subdue those baser instincts of the physical or lower-self, the better man is inclined to yield to the illuminating wisdom of the Divine prerogatives.

# Chapter Eight:  The Balanced Life

*"I brought you everything it takes to save a nation,*
*now take it, and save yourself..."*

When the Prophet reportedly spoke those words to the
Moorish Americans, he is said to have been holding up
a circle seven Koran of the M.S.T. of A. and a
questionnaire, the primary sources of instruction used
in the temple's public teachings and meetings.

Ali designated his doctrine "Islamism", perhaps for
various reasons, to distinguish it from the religious
practices and cultural tradition of the Arabian desert.
Neither did he come with the revelation of the Prophet
Mohammed, whose work was to destroy the idolatry
of the tribes of Ishmael, and restore the original
submissive spirit of Adam to the
life and religion of men.

Each is an instance for good to the purest faith, that
doctrine of the progressive illumination of the human
spirit, investiture with sacred knowledge, even divine
use of the imperfect vehicles of religious faith.

The diligent student of wisdom would rightly infer
that Ali had assimilated the teachings of ancient

mysticism, divine knowledge , sacred wisdom, held by the interrelated esoteric traditions that include West Africa to Egypt, Nubia, and Ethiopia, even as far as India and of course the arcanum of the Arabian desert, then delicately concealed that information in his cryptic instructions and keys to the Moorish theology.

The visit of the Greek historian Herodotus, to those most ancient Temples of Egypt around 500 BC, where he is reportedly taught by the priests, that their history exceeded 17,000 years, and was introduced to records well preserved and recorded in successive unbroken periods of 330 kings and 300 priests. He further testifies that all of their knowledge and the mysteries of their religion where memorized by the priesthood.

Before there was one king or pharaoh of Egypt, it is recorded that the people were ruled by seven gods by whom they were taught their peculiar religion, arts and sciences, and Menes their first king, changed the course of the Nile and built the great capital of Memphis on the recovered land.

Their ancient wisdom, and their religious mysteries had sustained and perpetuated for countless millennium, a civilization that was from all appearances born in the most remote periods of antiquity and to whom the entire Greek world at that time, were considered but children.

By this knowledge they conducted all of their affairs, determined their social interactions, influenced the intelligence and governed the lives of their people.

They understood the common and extraordinary usages of the sacred sciences, and that unceasing watchfulness should be maintained in the mind, the place of the scull, where the holy thought was first rejected, crucified, executed, and buried in a dark grave of earthly passions and desires.

In truth, the end of this life's work and purpose, is not mere acquisition of material wealth, mere acquisition of physical things is verily the end of true life.

The true adept, is not so immediately but rather is enlightened by measure, and raised by degree until he is perfected. Unlike other orders, in Moorish teaching, it is not in the labor of man that his soul is perfected or his heart made pure, but one's being in the hands of the ever-living Master Builder.

Even so there is that requisite balance between the inner life and the outer life, physical and spiritual, the heavenly and the worldly, a place for each and each in its place, neither is it ever of any benefit to confuse the two.

A well balanced life requires a daily commitment in each of several vital areas, without which one's life may become cluttered, confusing and overwhelming in its constant demands.

This often presents more than a few problems for members of the African American community, normally disproportionally lacking the social skills or intellectual tools  needed to build solid, stable well composed lives.

The square, being a tool used to measure right angles, when used in conjunction with the compass demonstrates two careful considerations in the taking of one definite action, or using several exact measurements to isolate a designated point.

For any work to be firmly established and enduring, symmetry must be the rule by which different parts are melded together to complete the perfected whole, the conciliation of all influences by equal and complementary influences.

There is taught in professor Drew's philosophical school of self discovery and divine knowledge, this science and the proper use of the various tools and other materials used in the construction of the the holy temple within the heart, Allah's meeting place with man.

*"See that thou build it according to the pattern that
was shown to thee in heaven".*

Each is individually, directly responsible for the
construction, or for that matter, the destruction of their
spiritual life and upkeep of the temple within.

" All of the tools are used where? In the workshop of
the mind, where things are made of thought ".

By reason and experience, the thinking and analytical
faculties are cultivated and perfected," made fit for the
master's use ".

It is discovered that there are two distinct natures in
men, two diametrically opposing tendencies, the lower
baser impulses of the physical nature, and the eternal
being, the spirit man, as passenger or director of his
necessary vehicles of locomotion and manifestation.

Every victory over self, is a plumbing of the walls,
fastening of the joints, securing of the doors and
cleaning the windows of the house. That the Sun, at
its highest point, is certain to enter in and illuminate
throughout and fill each and every room.

In the way of life and light, it is the builder's labor

with sincere and conscious effort to exalt and work in his true self with authority and power over illusionary and carnal life.

It is the higher self, in conscious knowledge of his being, acting and reciprocating in all the affairs of his earthly and extra dimensional existence. Having a just balance and a fair equilibrium between mundane life and the holy endeavors of the spiritual realms.

The carnal man, severely restricted by the darkness, deceit, and disinformation of the lower-self, facilitates his own misleading and faulty understanding or interpretation of the true light.

The true explications are reserved for those that are proven faithful, the divine right of every one with proper birth into the kingdoms above.

That well balanced man has discovered it to be advantageous, to suppose himself neither good nor evil but rather to be neither, having unfeigned stability in public and private, always of a clear mind , with distinguished purposes. True wisdom, which clearly comprehends and consistently employs the ages old adage that, " there is a time and a purpose for everything under heaven".

Such as have learned to be themselves without effort,

reposed, resilient, resting comfortably in one's own personality and character type.

Ever considering, that for every action there is of necessity an equal and opposite reaction, subsequently, all true master men, " revealers " of the light, strive to maintain invariant consciousness of Holy breath, that which was, is and ever-more to be. Amen.

# Chapter Nine:  The Message and the Messengers

*"...the gods have spoken to the Greek, and kindred tongues, through images made by man, but Allah the One now speaks to man........not by an oracle made of wood and gold, but by the voice of man...".*

Throughout the history of humanity there have ever been prophets, teachers, mystics, masters and divines, who have communicated the messages from the heaven realm to men.  In every land there exist some sacred doctrine used to elevate the mind and hearts of the people and turn them away from sin.

All true and divine messengers, prophets, priest, sages, teachers and mystics, are emissaries from the other realms, of the same spirit, co-workers, and fellow laborers

As the nations have ever engaged in the business of commerce and trade, so there has also ever been the exchange of religious belief, philosophies and ideas.

Religious belief systems and practices, for the most part spread, east to west, east from Egypt and the fertile crescent of the Middle East.  Also from that

118

point the ancient wisdom, sacred sciences, and mystery systems or schools of instruction and initiation.

It was ageless Khamet (Egypt), that nourished the schools of Greece, generated her mythology and philosophy and instructed the famed Greek minds Socrates to Philo, Herodotus to Pythagoras, all traveled to Egypt to receive instruction and training in the sacred sciences

Every messenger's life energies are wrapped up in the ultimate concern of carrying out the work and taking care of the responsibilities that the Almighty has placed in their care.

The prophets of olden times, in every land and from every people were more than living oracles to the multitudes, they were mystics, and master-minds as well, who investigated the composition of man and matter, the invisible realms and the manifested Powers of nature, all universally agreeing in essence that, "God is light, and in Him is no darkness and all".

But for a brief moment in time, the spiritual messengers live and work on this plane, yet, their words reverberate across the eons of time, impacting the lives, raising the consciousness of untold numbers, for unknown generations to come.

119

Those without the light of an informed and illuminating intelligence, are held in a state ( or condition) real or imagined, of mental bondage, confusion, and distorted views of life. The thoughts of such men are held to the basest levels, concerned with only the lowest instincts of mere survival and physical gratification.

We need desperately to hear again the voices of our predecessors, calling us to another resurrection, the rising body of the indomitable old African. In these times we need their insight, their wisdom and fierce determination.

It was the voice of the honorable Marcus Garvey, who clearly explained why the Black man in America faces unrelenting hatred, when he said, "...teach your children, that they are direct descendants of the greatest and proudest race who ever peopled the earth; and it is because of the fear of our return to power, in a civilization of our own, that might outshine others, that we are hated and kept down by a jealous and prejudiced contemporary world..."

The Noble prophet Drew Ali in another vein said," A beggar people cannot develop the highest in them, nor can they attain to a genuine enjoyment of the spiritualities of life ". He emphasized the necessity that we support and uplift each other practically as well, when he said in addition, *"...we have many men and women among our people who are qualified, both by training and experience, are shining lights in the business world of all people. It is a sad weakness in us, as a people, that we have withheld the very encouragement, support and patronage that would have made some of our worthy business ventures a grand success. And worst of all, have joined in the condemnations of them when they failed ".*

*" Except in cases of actual dishonesty, discourtesy, lack of service and actual unreliability, our business enterprises in every field of endeavor should have fullest of confidence, cooperation and patronage whenever and wherever they can be given ".*

In one Moorish document Ali teaches, "...the problems of life are largely social and economic. In a profound sense, they are moral and spiritual ". Over much emphasis can be placed on nationality, or historical identity, at the expense of tangible, much needed and positives changes, real progress, beneficial, actual achievements in the uplifting of ourselves and our people.

At the root, the problem is a spiritual problem, a psychological dilemma that must be overcome and of course there is still too much religious controversy as to the right thing.

121

The history of Black America's struggle in this
country, is clearly defined and best understood through
the history of the different religious and ethnic
movements, organizations and outstanding
personalities that have worked to direct the
advancement and uplifting of our people in this
African Diaspora. These have been our messengers,
our luminaries , our prophets.

God has sent to every oppressed and downtrodden
people, messengers, and guides, Ali likewise
proclaimed as his  source of internal inspiration and
revelation, the same as given to all true and divine
prophets.

As in other lands and other struggles, we have also our
list of notable and influential leaders that reads like a
book of martyrs.

Despite the thoughts, desires, or ill wishes of many,
we are no less people, that the Eternal should not give
thought to our plight.

Most of us are able to understand how the efforts of
these men and women were compatible with and part
of the "great work", as the overall stratagem for the
elevation and illumination of the human race.  No
mass movements of any sort can be maintained

without the assistance of like minded persons outside as well as inside.

Among our first duties, is the commitment to the uplifting of ourselves, that we first need to be better citizens, productive and industrious members of society. If we are found to be doing otherwise, we are not acting in the best interest of ourselves or the people around us. We all have the potential should we choose to use it, to rise above our present conditions " to dare and to do wondrous things".

Our collective wisdom and practical knowledge gained from our experiences, can be seen most clearly in the visions of freedom that many of our past leaders have etched for us on the walls of time, memorials to the unforgettable sacrifices they made, in order to inspire and encourage us to continued and complete this difficult journey.

## Chapter Ten:   To set the Captives Free

Perhaps, it is in youth that freedom is best appreciated and put to use, even if not perfectly understood, it may be that age of innocence we try so desperately to reclaim.

Freedom is a word that carries with it a tremendous weight of responsibility, there is the implication of one that is consciously aware of the various demands and circumstances which life presents, and diligently directs his thoughts and energies in the most prudent, conscientious manner possible.

Any free society that allows a public persecution in any form or condones aggressive unwarranted intolerance against any of its citizens, is not entitled to the name of free.

If we would be just, we would do more than merely tolerate those who differ from our selves, but recognizing and openly acknowledging, the rights of all men to freedom, justice, and equality.

We should in fact, take a fresh look at our history, from the history of Western Africa, south and east of the continent, Egypt, Ethiopia, Nubia, and soberly

consider our connections and contributions to many of
the worlds great, often unsurpassed civilizations.
Never to forget the dark passage through the belly of
the beast, America's unique slavery institution. A lot
that fell to millions of Africa's children.

This generation is the product of that fiery trial, having
come out of the iron furnace, from open oppression
and abuse, far too many of our people are yet without
an appreciable idea, of just who we are, where we
have been, or who our forefathers were.

Does it really matter? Would any difference be made
if we did know?  Just look at some of the differences
between " White America " and " Black America ",
their historical self-images, public designation or
descriptions, overall success or failure as a group, as
well as their different depiction and representation of
themselves (and others), in movies, novels, etc., then
reconsider that question.

Self determination, and self perception, operate hand
in hand, equally with the elevation and advancement
of a people, as well as the degradation or destruction
of one.

Every group and nation maintains its historical record,
it's sacred values and traditions, memorialized
in its unique and particular rituals and archives of

125

events, records, keys of knowledge and of wisdom, all
traditions and legal systems.

Throughout the human family, with every religious
sect, every major and minor belief system, whether
orthodox or UN-orthodox, Jew, Muslim, Sikh,
Christian, or virtually unknowns, all true and divine
religions of the world that recognize a Supreme
Divinity, share faith in an unseen world of eternity,
operate within some form of systematized order of
study, ceremony, ritual, and worship, likewise all have
their different scriptures, Holy books, records of
sacred inspiration, communications and divine
illuminations.

The Moorish-Americans, though they openly
acknowledge the Revelations of all true and Divine
Prophets, i.e., Jesus, Buddha, Confucius, and
Mohammed, will usually deal more consistently with
the esoteric aspect of the various doctrines to discover
as much of the original import as possible and it's
relevant connection and application in the sacred
sciences.

It is from the Holy Qur'an of Mecca, that the Prophet
is said to derive his power and authority,
consequentially, he compiled a book of instructions,
especially suited to use by the Moorish-Americans, to
change their perception and use of religion and

religious history.

A master adept and divine minister, should be able to compile a Manual of instruction from the comics section of a daily newspaper, understanding all designed, intended and possible effects on the thought processes particularly on novices and young aspirants.

Psychology is the science of dealing with the mind and with the mental and emotional processes. This area of study and expertise must of necessity have been in some form or another, from the beginning, a part of spiritual and religious, philosophic practices.

The carnal mind, lower-self, the body of uncontrolled desires, by its nature gravitates toward darkness, be it the absence of physical light, lack of intellectual illumination, or a state of spiritual confusion.

*"A master never screens himself for the sake of reputation or fame...."*

A true master of the light, irregardless of his affiliation, be it a Moorish, Masonic, Christine, Philosophic, or whatever persuasion, can not without directly contradicting, his moral compass, dismiss the light whenever it may manifest it's presence, or who, it by divine providence, should manifest through.

127

The demeaning arrogance, coupled with growing incompetence of many exclusively American fraternal or religious societies, with their steadily declining memberships and relevance, may prove opportunistic for other contemporary groups. Once again, the popular imagination must be readjusted to more clearly conceive and receive the ancient wisdom, to consciously perpetuate the mass initiatory process along the path to regeneration of the human family.

One of histories most unique and fascinating threads is that of the western religious guilds, the eastern brotherhoods, mystical orders or other such groups that find place in recorded history. From the arcane priesthood of Egypt to the college of Adepts in the Northwest, the Essence of the Palestinian Deserts, or the old testament school of the Prophets, everywhere beyond the din of everyday life, in solitude and silent work, the arcane traditions of initiation and progression, continuous, from the earliest known cultural traditions, assisting men into the presence of the Infinite.

In the most remote regions of the earth, in tropical Africa or the jungles of South America, with the aboriginals in the outback of Australia, from among the least civilized to the most modernized nations of the world, men and women travel the paths to the arcane temple, the holy house of wisdom.

Schools of life and light will come as long as
humanity travels on this lower plane of life. Prophets
and holy men and women will continue teaching us
how to know the truth, how to put it into practice, and
overcome the carnal nature or lower-self, how we can
manifest the higher self, the god within and be the best
that we have the potential to be.

Every true and divine religion has its external shell of
religious practices, ceremony, ritual and dogma, as
well as its esoteric core. Most people are content to
appropriate the outer garments of religious faith or
other type of association, indicative of spiritual life,
insight and awareness, rather than pay the actual price
of practice and acquisition.

Freedom, justice, and equality for many, has been like
unto the recovery of an unknown treasure, that has
been well buried in the ground, hidden under the very
feet of men and women who are toiling every day of
life, with no relief in sight, never dreaming that just
below the surface of mundane life, is the hidden way,
the key to the very life that they seek.

This is what is meant, that man must earn his way " by
the sweat of his brow ", implying more than physical
labor to meet the needs of ordinary life, but by the

development as well of his mind, his mental faculties and the purifying of his heart.

Even so, that liberty divinely bestowed on all men, is ever threatened, it's right manipulated by powerful governments and unchecked ecclesiastical monstrosities. What religion is that, which forces itself in the lives of men and collects its tribute through fear?

We are of course as strong as our weakest link, and the work of master minds in every age is the uplifting of fallen humanity.

It is a worldwide and concerted effort rather than the work of any single group or entity.

By various means of religious or cultural expressions, employing the same basic concepts to continuously elevate the consciousness in the life of all men.

With hundreds of millions of people living in this advanced civilization, there are still a select few who somehow are yet convinced that they are superior above all others, usually because of their appearance. They believe themselves entitled to special privileges, and place little, if any value, on the rights and lives of any unlike themselves.

The ideas of competition, accumulation, even basic survival and self preservation have been distorted beyond recognition, especially here in the west, we have created our own box and not only insist on living in it, but that the world around us do so as well.

How many millions, tightly cocooned in self-created delusions, becoming less sensitive daily, of the increasingly shocking realities happening all over the world.

We should concern ourselves with the things that matter, the real essence of life in America, a clear conception of what works for the overall betterment of our conditions, what makes meaningful, useful, substantive contributions to society.

For those that are living in these days, we are the people born for this hour, we are the answer that we had been hoping would come. These are challenges that will bring forth the latent potential resident in all of us. Learning to live life, and increase in life by the power in the untapped reservoir of the ancient wisdom, our forefathers' vast estate.

To finally overcome, we must look squarely at our true history, the complete history beyond even the beginnings of this country, and look honestly at ourselves. It is we, that must reconcile ourselves with the fact that there is yet much to be done, and that we owe it to all who preceded us, more importantly, to our children and ourselves, to repair the torn legacy of our ancestral heritage.

To divest ourselves, not merely of the names that delude to slavery, to being less than, to being others peoples idea and definitions, but to refuse as well everything that those names historically represent, according to the opinions, definitions, and determinations of the dominant society.

It is well settled for many, that there is indeed access to a more precise means of knowing life, of discovering truth, of perceiving the proper course of action.

What we are in fact learning, is what affects the way people think and why, the varying circumstances in life, and the powers at play in the often conflicting circumstances. All that make up the world of good and not so good, even the machinations of the universe, of man and his process of becoming, the mystery of God, of life after death and the quest for immortality.

*"...he opened up the prison doors and set the prisoners free.  He broke the chains of captive souls, and led the captives to the light..."*

## Chapter Eleven:   The Bonds of Brotherhood

*"...from olden times it was ordained that you should be with us, and in this sacred school be taught."*

One thing that some Moorish-Americans, Black Muslims, Black nationalist, and other African-American fraternal, esoteric or secret social groups seem unprepared or unwilling to accept, is that western freemasonry, through their Potentates, rulers, and hierarchical leadership, maintains established 'ties' with African, Arabian, Indian and other eastern mystic orders and societies, interlocked in a world-wide network and fellowship in the ancient wisdom traditions.

In actuality, there is a global network of spiritual fellowships, religious participation, sacred to secret societies, silent brotherhoods, fraternal and religious orders. Most in the tradition of the sons of light, while others choose the dark or left-hand path. These schools of thought span the ages, under-girding the faith of man, maintaining the knowledge of God, perfecting the science of penetration into the Infinite.

From Egypt, the name by which the Greeks, the adopted children of the Egyptian priesthood, called the mystical land of the Pharaohs, sprang all the mystery tradition and sacred sciences of man and creation.

Even India, with its ancient temples and memorials, It's sacred traditions and holy wisdom, based on the Rig Veda, which can be traced back to 1500 years BC, is derived from the land of the pyramids.

There are also among the brotherhoods of Africa, those that trace their origins to the dynasty of Cheops ( Khufu ), predating by thousands of years, many of today's such traditions.

A land of mystery and riddles, Egypt, even in its first recorded periods, appeared ancient in contrast with her contemporary nations, kingdoms, etc., and was complete with advanced administration of government, the cultivation of all known arts and sciences.

It was often difficult, and for most impossible, to gain admission into many of the ancient orders, some requiring more than seven years of waiting to be considered, others, that all earthly possessions as well as family and friends be dispensed with, not to mention the difficult tests and trials that attended every step in advancement, often increasing in intensity as well.

The unfit, insincere and defective character types were thereby easily and efficiently eliminated, neither has any ever penetrated into the sanctum sanctorum, the most sacred of the inner mysteries.

When the great Library of Alexandria was sacked and burned by the barbarian hordes, the most precious and sacred documents or other materials pertaining to the secret doctrines, were buried in the desert, in the vast northwest. Though centuries have past, the lines of succession in the hierophants and masters of the sacred schools have continued unbroken, and the great work unceasing.

Ridiculed and rejected by polite society, these, from every walk of life, study their "controversial sciences" in the prudence of silence; the ages old wisdom, the sacred doctrine, built on the foundational doctrines of the Fatherhood of God, the brotherhood of all men, and the immortality of the soul. Even so seekers and travelers continue their spiritual quest, knowing that behind every religious tradition, there is the more spiritual aspect of teachings and practical experience,

The mystical side of the Islamic religion, Sufism, consists of various groups of Muslim brotherhoods, each having their own customs, manners, and secret knowledge, organized to some extent in the manner borrowed by western freemasonry with different levels, rituals, and degrees of enlightenment.

All across the Arabic speaking world, where the faith of Islam is acknowledged in any significant measure, there is likely also to be some semblance of mystic thought or doctrine that will find origins in the Sufi traditions.

The hidden knowledge of Sufism predates itself any organized Sufi brotherhoods, as they were formed after the revelations to Mohammed ignited the new faith.

Initiates into the secrets of nature, man, and God have traversed for thousands of years, the paths that lead to ancient Egypt, Ethiopia, and India, even Mecca has been a center for learning in occult sciences, producing its adepts likewise far back into recorded time.

We should be extremely careful in labeling or judging any group, person, or member of any organization, even based on the actions of the few, not painting everyone with the same brush, or putting all people of any persuasion in the same category, we are much wiser than that.

*"But by their fruit, you shall know them..."*

By their fruit, by what they produce, because action always speak louder than words, our actions not only define us, they speak for us and about as as well.

The real reason a Black man cannot be a free -mason in the western tradition is simple, he would be imitating himself, he would be pretending to be his own ancestors, which is really what others are doing.

An almost insurmountable obstacle, is that western or European masonry was originally designed for Europeans, a western interpretation in the Christine expression, made for a particular people having common customs and ancestry, cultural and historical viewpoints according to their particular schools of thought. The mysteries of philosophical and metaphysical light were communicated through a Christian system of symbols, metaphors, allegory, and legends.

To properly interpret the lessons required for the most part a Eurocentric world view and vantage point. Though there is nothing in any of the degrees teaching or espousing racism, hatred or prejudicial treatment, that did not prevent a historical denial of " brotherly love" toward anyone in America not considered "white".
The Essence may be described as a brotherhood of prophets and holy men who lived an aesthetic life in

devotion to the spiritual life, separated by their way of life and the Jude-an desert from the rest of ancient Israel. They are believed by some scholars, to have been connected with or the same as the Qumran community that wrote the now famous Dead Sea scrolls and existed between 120 B.C. and 70 A.D.

One of the scrolls contain prophecy, written around 100 years before the coming of Jesus, prophesying the coming of the teacher of righteousness, of his birth, life, and death, while another speaks of the war between "the sons of light" and the "sons of darkness". The old prophets, and seers welcomed the one who would open up the age of the kingdom of life, light, and love divine.

The silent brotherhoods have dwelt for generations in the deserts and wastelands of near and further east, even as other brothers throughout the antediluvian world waited and worked toward the spiritual restoration of the human race.

It was they who preserved the sacred knowledge and wisdom from the antediluvian world, their teachings handed down through their masters, wise men and hierophants.

The original of the Christine faith, were in many respects a secret society, having their own sacred doctrine, symbols, signs and passwords, only those found faithful were admitted to the circle of adepts, usually the Elders clothed in white garments.

Man is a composite being, his inner life is often in conflict with his outward personality, the fixed is solved when man himself, the spirit man, the higher self, is seated on the throne of decisive power.

The lower mind, the carnal mind, with its body of desires, must be made subservient to the will of the Higher self, by the conscious control of the thought productive faculties. The elaborate ceremonies, ancient rituals, memorization of sacred text, oral histories and other ascetic practices, all worked together to produce in the devotee, a constant re-ordering and purifying of the psyche, purifying of the heart, and the silent building of the inner temple for the truth.

When art is mentioned, most will think of some great painting, statue, or other such creative work, yet the most original definition for and use of the word was descriptive of skill, technical knowledge, and proficiency or expertise in the exercise and practical application of the divine wisdom.

Initially, the word craft, as in a masonic usage, concerned skill and knowledge of a particular worker in a given field of building construction, it came to represent symbolically skill and proficiency and knowledge in a certain measure or degree.

The word science originally carried the same implication as being an art or craft, it was used to designate an area or branch of investigation, research, and learning.
We are all held bound together by the mystic tie of life, of light and the will of the Omnipotent and by the mystery of death are we initiated into those greater mysteries of existence.

The concept of a "thought of Allah manifested in the flesh", represents a different ideological paradigm for a new age. The old garments that once clothed the considerable light, have worn out, become unfruitful, static, and ineffective in purpose. The sacred teachings are activating ingredients and must be lived or acted out to be actualized.

Therefore, it is for that cause that Drew Ali gave the Moorish-Americans the directive to " imitate I the Prophet ", as he acted out the life, light and mind of a resurrected Moorish-American, one who had been literally, and figuratively slain and buried in the west, in a shallow grave, raised again to life, light and consciousness.

## Chapter Twelve:   The  Builders of Men

*"...He found the object of his search engaged in
building dwellings for the sons of men..."*

Siddhartha Gautama, the great enlightened one of
India, is much thought to be Her greatest and most
significant gift to civilization.  Slightly less than 600
years before the birth of Christ, this great moral,
spiritual, and philosophical legislator transformed an
entire continent with a blazing light.  Like most of the
world's great religions, the original form of Buddhism
was simple and direct, " There are two extremes which
should be avoided ".

Alluding to a living of over much pleasure, or a life
miserable and vain.  The masses made a god of one
who instead was a living oracle of the Holy One.

The honorable Chinese philosopher Lao Tzu, from
whom, the doctrine of Taoism was derived, made
interesting and astute observations about man and
society, or further, society's affects on men. Tao was
named "the way", and Lao Tzu taught that man must
rediscover his original nature, to be free of
aggressiveness, competitiveness, and immorality.

141

He believed that society could become a great
reservoir of aggressive, competitive persons used to
fund, as it were, a state financed conquering military,
an overly competitive and aggressive business climate,
a hostile society continually producing children even
more extreme than themselves.

Though inspired for the moment, the inattentive nature
of men over time erodes twice the accomplishments of
their massive social, religious, or political movements,
normally engendering unprecedented changes.

It remains the more exclusive interest of those that
have an innate, an insatiable desire to investigate and
inquire into the various schools of alternative thought
and spiritual verities.

*"And where science and philosophy fail, where the
brief finite reason of man faltered and turned blind in
the presence of infinity, faith might mount to the feet
of God by ascetic discipline, unselfish devotion, the
unconditional surrender of the part to the whole."*

*" He that leaves his home in search of knowledge
walks in the path of God ".*

Perhaps it was stifling heat, the inescapable assault of
one of the most consistently hot and humid inhabited

142

areas on Earth, and the most populous one as well, that caused the country of India to produce more ascetics, than comparatively any other people in the world.

The yogi or holy men, of India, its strangest, most defining expression, their often strange and extreme disciplines, unimaginable self denial, and abstinence, free the soul, and release it to experience a type of union with the Supreme.

For at the least the last 2500 years, and possibly unto the most remote periods, fair numbers of these type of aesthetic mystics, and savants, have been an inseparable part of the Indian life and culture.

Yet, even within the practices of yoga, the sought after enlightenment was not in any case obtained immediately, but rather the seeker would advance in stages, and step by step, in measure of understanding.

The mysticism of India, Egypt, and Palestine greatly influenced its development in the Arabic world at least a few millennium ago, it was the pious minority, concerned more with the spiritual aspects of religion, rather than its economic or other interest

Always among them, a few were inclined to completely denounce the world, and were completely

143

given over to pursuit of the mystical, alternative states of reality.

Being the most likely to insist on maintaining pristine adherence to the original revelations, they resented any obstacle, especially human, between themselves and unity with godhead.

Very reminiscent of the brotherhood in the desert regions of the dead sea, where the dead sea scrolls were found in 1947, the early Sufi brotherhoods formed into mystical bodies, with several levels of training and knowledge.

Their name was taken from the simple robe of wool ( suf ) that was worn by the devotee, and they had a complete course of disciplines they held as necessary to the illuminating experience, the mystical revelation of God.

Among their oldest doctrines, is the teaching that, the knowledge of God is in the heart of man, and it could only be found, by abandoning earthly desires, and focusing instead on that which is everlasting.

Mysticism among Islamic sects and people has a continuous history thousands of years before the advent of the Prophet Mohammed, Mecca itself being a center of religious worship, crossroads of the east, as well as center of trade and commerce, hundreds of years previous to the revelations to the Prophet, engaging also in diplomatic relationships and trade with Egypt, Greece, Persia and India.

Arabia's mystery schools maintained relationships as well with Egypt and India, and there is evidence of a well ordered tradition of intercourse between the various sacred schools that existed in practically every community, in some variation, by the networking of traveling mystics, holy men, philosophers, and sages, which was well-maintained throughout the inhabited world as far back as we have recorded history.

All of the northern half of Africa were well acquainted with the Egyptian mystery system thousands of years ago and some regions were old enough to have ancient philosophical and initiating systems of their own. This in part explains the swift practically non-violent conversion of the northern half of the continent during the western march of the Islamic conquest.

The established as well as the nomadic tribes of the great African northwest, quickly assimilated the mysteries of Islam, along with the daily practices of the Faith. From Egypt, across the entire expanse including all of the Barbary states, the kingdom of Morocco, all of Fezzan, to the furthest reaches of the great Niger River, all to some extent or other shared the Noble Moorish Science, religious faith, and culture.

As such, it was then the Moorish adepts of northwest, the sages of the desert lands, wandering marabouts, mystics, sages and holy men, traveling the height and dept, midst and breadth of Mother Africa. The Moors became, at the imminent decline of Egypt, became in fact and theory, the last true custodians of her mysteries.

Adept implies long successful experience, expansive knowledge of the sacred sciences, practical knowledge of the ancient wisdom, one who is a recognized authority on esoteric, mystical, religious, philosophical, or occult subjects.

In the world of antiquity, an adept was known as a god among men, perfected in the sacred schools, such a one was thought to have mastered the known arts and sciences, ascended to the realms of the gods, endured the most excruciating test and ordeals, and as his reward, received divine illumination and investment with supreme wisdom. Thus, he was afterward known as a twice born man, beholder of the eternal and of royal statue, equal among princes.

Some confusion often comes about, when the word " free-mason ", is used generally, to describe every order, sacred school, or brotherhood, many of which have existed hundreds if not thousands of years prior to the formation of that organization in 1717 A.D.

Most prestigious among Black America's secret societies is the Masonic body known as the Prince Hall free and accepted masons, noting that there are other bodies, with their own particular grand lodges, jurisdictions, etc.,

However, Prince Hall generally considers practically all other bodies of black masons as being "clandestine", even as they themselves have lamented their unjust treatment, and the exact same consideration of being "clandestine " by all but the entirety of the "white" Masonic family and organizational superstructure. (with the exception of recent official nods of recognition from a few grand lodges).

But in today's light, we find that the order of American Masonry is likewise considered an aberration, by certain European Shriners and " brotherhoods of the east ", however, the more "noble" of the American Shrine, may actually be accepted by them as a move of the west back to what they consider as " the true brotherhood " and the return to " true freemasonry " as descended from their " true Grand Master, Enoch ".

147

It may appear in the final analysis, that the " Ancient Egyptian Arabic Order of Nobles ", as the Black Shriners were called, in what was for them to a great extent an unveiling of their actual lost history, culture, and sacred traditions, stepped to the forefront in the American version of freemasonry with what is often described as a more serious, studious " approach towards the East ".

Founded slightly less than thirty years from the Emancipation (1893), it is certainly conceivable that the " Black Shriners ", in a search for real freedom and equality, found in the masonic philosophy, especially the keys to their degree, the door to the "continuing of their masonic education", the location of the true light, the primary object of every sincere "traveler's" journey, more importantly, clues to the lost history and identities of their people.

Interesting parallels in philosophical and ideological thought are quite apparent, between freemasonry, the mystic orders of ancient Islam, Sufi sects, and the ascetic and religious orders of the east. When such points are raised, or their similarities highlighted, it becomes obvious that the entire body of western freemasonry is to some extent an appendage of eastern philosophical, mystical, occult thought and practice.

Even those arcane brotherhoods and sacred orders of

148

the east and the mystical African Northwest, sprang from dramatic historical events, mystical and religious experiences, and to a chosen few, divine revelation.

Throughout the most remote periods of history, real and legendary events have been transformed into parables, allegories, myths, legends or illustrative instructions in the great mysteries of life and the ages.

The beloved and popular Ali, the son-in-law of Mohammed, never lived to fulfill the position of the Caliphate, he fell at Kerbela, assassinated by a poisoned sword from among a group of rebels ( the Kharijites ) , the victim of a conspiracy to usurp the seat of Islamic power.

The spot where Ali died became a holy place to the Shia sect, his shrine became the goal of pilgrimage almost as sacred as the journey to Mecca.

Egypt, the Capital empire of the dominion of Amexem ( Africa ), is fixed and established in the northeast corner of the greater continent, and has been as such, the foundational stone on which Africa's entire history, the histories of Her people around the world, have rested since time immemorial.

Which is particularly interesting, given the position of the candidate for initiations as in the northeast, and

149

from there begins his journey towards the east, in search of truth and light.

A few miscellaneous sects teach that the true master workman, never leaves the north-east position, there, he being in a perfectly balanced position to carry out his appointed labor between this world and the next.

Having began in absolute darkness, according to the days of his heart, a move to the light which he is never completely in, according to an absolute sense of things, he must still attend to the affairs of this life. Thus this is where he finds himself, until the Master of the Universe so determines his work to be completed.

With the Moors, the greater northwest, in fact present day portions of North America, held significant import. For some it was an extension and part of an ancient empire that spanned from the river Niger, northwest across the great Atlantis, to present day portions of north, south, and central America.

Still considered as unacceptable in " respected " fields of historical research, information tending to confirm the existence of history beneath the history and civilizations more highly enlightened, and technologically advanced than we, with our "information age " could possibly fathom, can quite literally be found in sacred documents, and archeological relics  discovered all around the world.

Perhaps it was an extensive knowledge of African-Asiatic history and cultural traditions, or knowledge generally unavailable to the public, that convinced Drew Ali so immutably, of those alternative accounts of history and  the truth of them.

It follows that as in the days of old, adepts during the time of Prophet Drew Ali, would be continuing in the same sacred traditions.

Ali's esoteric doctrine of Islamism, is made a contemporary transmission of the age old wisdom through the vehicle of his religious organizations religious and philosophical doctrine.

Of course, Drew Ali was also an apparently a well educated man, perhaps a self taught scholar, as many African Americans were doing that time, giving due consideration to his tremendous accomplishments.  It follows then, that he would have done nothing without serious consideration of the possible impact or interpretations.

In adding the suffix 'ism', to the word Islam, which universally is accepted as meaning, "submission to the will of God", the objective being to encourage the Moorish adherents to engage in the science, or practice of the spiritual, philosophical, and intellectual approach to religion.

With that thought methodology, we may use two more precise mathematical tools to pinpoint an exact location. The idea, after which is the manifest,  in measure stages, along one of the processes of becoming.

The information is clear and concise, the inference should naturally come that the information is to suggest, that the divine knowledge must first be used in the thought-life.

## Chapter Thirteen:  The Fatherhood of God

*" All people worship Allah the One; but all the people
see him not alike....man names the part of Allah he
sees, and this to him is all of Allah....when man sees
Allah as one with him, he goes straight up to Him, and
says, " My Father-God-Allah "...... the one who
everywhere... is the causeless cause, the rootless root,
from which are things have grown..."*

In that light, should all be inspired to return to his or
her particular house of worship, particular faith, or
practices, with renewed energy, devotion and
determination.

Likewise, the heart of one's soul purified, absent any
intolerance, prejudice or the like, can clearly see
as if before the throne and holy altar of Heaven, all
humanity, dependent on the Divine care.

Thereby we know that it is the Father alone, Holy and
transcendent, that "calleth forth worlds by the words of
his mouth".

The pupil is capable of learning as soon as the teacher
is capable and prepared to teach, and it is only when

153

the student is prepared that the Master will come.

We would do well to be mindful that the great God in his dealings with us, does so according to our respective levels of growth and spiritual development.

When people are in darkness and afraid of the Eternal One, they mistake Him for an enemy or a foe, then dress up other men in fancy garbs and charged them to restrain His wrath, and so the way is open for carnal minded men to take full advantage of others, to " slouch under the wings of their cross ", and coldly extract from those that come to them, " the means whereby they may enjoy all the pleasures of this life ".

....... Those are they who serve gods that are " but demons in disguise ".....

What God would bestow life, with all of it's promising possibilities, to be amused by the sufferings, trials, and the deaths of mere mortals?

The iron handed oppression of many of today's established, accepted, organized religions, make it necessary for a devotee to conceal any experience or knowledge that could be considered controversial, and departing from the approved doctrines, or belief systems.

The wild masses of common people have always misunderstood, misrepresented, and misused religion, and they probably always will. How many senseless acts are perpetrated every day, how many precious lives are taken away, or communities, groups, and nations around the world live wretched, miserable lives, under the heel of some mad tyrannical dictator or other power hungry individuals, all drunk on some strange wine, that they call religion.

Perhaps it is for this reason that Noble Drew Ali made it a point to state in the September 14th, 1928 edition of "the Moorish Guide", concerning the religious faith of the Moors," We believe in the principals of its teachings (the Moslem religion), insofar as they can be adapted to American Life".

When taken together with the Prophet's " Warnings to all Moslems" (January 15 1929), when he informed "all members" that they must "end all radical, agitating speeches, while at work, in their homes, or on the streets". It is immediately apparent that there were more than a few Moors that either did not understand Ali's basic message, or completely disregarded the teachings of the Moorish prophet.

When and where ever, the Father has chosen through

selected messengers, to communicate to humanity His willingness and conditions for a spiritual relationship with the creatures of his hand, some power mad finite human beings are not long to declare themselves the only means of a relationship with the eternal, and that all men must give heed to them alone or be banished from the presence of God.

Rarely does any one person or group, comprehend and appreciate the messages of Heaven in the fundamental truths found in all true religions creeds, respecting the divine right of every man and woman to worship and follow the dictates of their own conscience and knowledge of that Holy one.

Neither is there any right, divine or otherwise, justifying the use of force or coercion against the will of others, to accept or practice any particular belief system.

*"...all people worship Allah, the One; but all the people see Him not alike...."*

To suppose that one individual may determine the value of another's life is insanity, to do so in the name of God or the cause of some religion is pure madness.

How many are in love with their own persuasions, their beliefs and conceptions of the Holy One, seemingly with little if any concern what He Himself many say to the contrary, they will stubbornly refuse to listen, but continue in the course determined by their own hearts.

In the few reliable documents, religious literature, or other extant materials, it is clear that Moorish Science's doctrine, as can be determined by the very words of the illustrious prophet, mandates moral rectitude, obedience to law, respect for government, recognition of the public and private rights of all people, yet there were and still are those who insist on deviating from the obvious, plain and clear teachings.

Drew Ali unleashed the power of freedom, especially religious freedom, he sought to use this power to make better citizens and more intelligent people, out of those who were the outcast of American society.

Only a true master, mature and perfected in the science of temple building is able to turn the power of his labor and the use of his tools to the great work of uplifting, preparing and equipping others.

Encouraged, by the knowledge of the absolute Father-hood of the one true God, and the brotherhood of all men, so he labors, knowing that he labors not alone or in vain, but with a great company of just men and women being likewise perfected.

However, as it has been historically, there was one understanding of the great faith of Ali for the intelligent, the educated, and enlightened who understand more clearly the prophet's message and mission, but to the uninformed or the insincere, they can only see opportunities to flaunt their new found knowledge, and to "treat whites with open contempt".

How plainly do we choose according to the truth of who and what we are inside, those who desire to learn, to grow, develop and reach their fullest potentials, make full and honest use of every opportunity of everyday life and strength is granted for them to do so.

Even our divisions, sometimes may serve the ultimate, the divine purpose. Can it be our religious differences also encourage the spiritual unfolding, the true evolution of the human race? Were we to agree, all of us in one earthly religious creed, would we lose the desire or perhaps not feel the need to inquire further?

Does the agitation of conflicting ideas, news, perspectives, vantage points and a fervent expression of them, demand that we pursue the more earnestly, certainty and absolute verification?

# Chapter Fourteen: Systematic and Symbolic Instructions

From our first conscious moments, we are beings that communicate by symbolic means, our articulated sounds and bodily gestures ever manifesting the mind of the thinking self. Interesting as well, our inner perceptive abilities, thinking, and reasoning faculties are stimulated by external stimuli that we interpret according to our understanding.

Even from the earliest civilizations various types of symbols have been used by different groups of people, to impart knowledge, information, and holy doctrine.

We all therefore have a natural acquaintance with symbolic methods of understanding abstract ideas, and philosophical concepts. Ceremonies and rituals common among all cultures are often expressions of human spiritual life and thought.

Anything may serve as a symbol that can be used as an outward sign of something abstract, immaterial, or invisible as well as certain thoughts, processes and concepts.

When applicable, each symbol, myth, parable,

allegory, even the personal spiritual experiences of the divine wisdom, is perceived by the individual, for the individual. Subsequently, there are therefore many possible interpretations, but only one correct interpretation, that insight however, can only be communicated by a symbol.

Our ability to not only thrive, but for most, to merely survive, is predicated and determined in no small measure by our ability to effectively understand and communicate with others through various symbolic forms.

To fully comprehend a symbol was to understand the instructions, likewise to thoroughly perceived the instruction is to apprehend the symbol.

In this light, we re-evaluate those things of which we have been previously convinced. It is only through the perpetuation and use of symbolism, that those precious truths have come to us in this present time. Perhaps because there has always been those who possess and rightly comprehended those secrets of God and nature, which they faithfully preserved and communicated to us in silent, symbolic form.

The sacred teachings of the mystery schools of antiquity, taught their most precious doctrines by symbols only and never was the sacred science effectively transmitted, but by such form or language. This form of communication and instruction, having emerged from beyond the mists of antiquity, survives as the only keys to the ancient Arcanum of the secret sciences.

Often it is as simple as looking at things just as they are to realize their import, message, and for whom any message may be intended.
Some wear rings on a particular finger or fingers, left or right hand, while others make use of medallions and other emblems on chains around their necks, or wear certain types of hats, headgear or other instruments.

We may error in looking far beyond the obvious meanings and messages being sent and subsequently become confused or worse mistaken by the varying and conflicting interpretations that become possible.

On the very front cover of the Moorish Koran, is the prominent symbol of the circle and seven, the first and obvious indication of how the contents are to be used, viewed, and comprehend, simply put, a symbolic book with symbolic instructions.

It is a masterfully correct compilation of philosophical, metaphysical alternatives, spiritualized views, and except for some historical material, the lessons are esoteric in nature and symbolically, rather than literally interpreted.

The Moors have often referred to it as their circle seven Koran, the character builder! When taken as such, it is a manual of instructions in moral conduct, a systematized means of discovery through parabolic, and divine truth, the true knowledge of Allah and man.

Life is the furnace, out of which are forged the various tools " we use in the workshop of the mind, where things are made of thought and where we build up character ".

The compass, level, and square, among the most essential of tools with which any skilled builder should become proficient, tools, which will be used from the design, to the actual construction or completion of any good work. Moreover, should the guiding hand of the Eternal, so direct our hearts and steps, in the building of a life in harmony with the divine (blueprint) plan, we labor to build true and erect, a holy temple for the truth.

The Holy instructions from the thought realm of purity and love, encourage the development of a particular rational, thought patterns, and intuitive faculties, all the block, joints and boards that go to complete that which life is spent to build.

There are two different aspects of life that we must reconcile, our public outer life, and our inner spiritual dimension, one will most certainly reflect accurately the other.

A major problem for many is that they are trying to understand two different systems , one that is built on European knowledge and degrees, and the second which is built on Afrocentric knowledge  and Asiatic degrees.

The European System is tailor made for people that are European in descent and worldview, therefore it presents great difficulties for people of other persuasions to comprehend and assimilate.
It would be as though one were trying to see light through another person's eyes.

Without the aid of some systematic or other forms of instruction, all would be left with the feeble and uncertain methods of trial and error in the development of our spiritual life.

*Yet, "...Man knows nothing by being told, he may believe what others say, but thus he never knows, if man would know he must himself be what he knows.....*

*Go to the desert my son; observe the young stork of the wilderness, let him speak to thy heart; he bareth on his wings his aged sire; he lodgeth him in safety and supplieth him with food..."*

The true wages of a real working master is knowledge and power to travel where he wills, to work in building up the lives of others with the knowledge of the truth, aiding and assisting those in need.

Those who rightly understand the process of spiritual maturity, of growth, of initiation, will likewise come to understand the means and methods of disseminating information and instructions by symbolic representation or veiled cryptic language.

Even our days, are of darkness as well as the light, a collection of cyclic measurements of time, of which, the sum total of our life experiences are comprised.

A circle is a revolution, a symbol of completion of an event or occurrence in a given period of time, also, in the perpetual motion of the universe, it's concourse with the unknown and the invisible elements, the circle is the symbol of eternity and timelessness.

On another plane of thought, the circle is the symbol of man, of his projects and designs, his aspirations, hopes and dreams, also of his failures, weaknesses, and doubts. To square the circle is the work of men, to better his conditions, to adapt his " inner life" to his physical conditions or earthly life, to bring his will in tune with the Deific Will, having a stable earthly life, yet in earnest pursuit of eternal verities.

The Khametian (Egyptian) initiates were taught and trained in the knowledge concerning the processes of natural events, the ebb and flow of the Nile, the seasons of rain or of planting and harvesting, they understood the power and potency of the sun.

The ancient mystery schools of the Nile, to which the children of Greece traveled in their infancy, to be suckled at the breast of Isis, till nourished enough to take the first unsteady steps toward civilization. It was above the entrance to the sacred schools of Khamet, where was first seen the words " know thyself ", by the famed Greek philosophers, who most western historians love to erroneously credit with having originated the saying.

But the ancients penetrated the starry sky as well, developed remarkably accurate charts of the positions and movements of visible objects, planets, stars, and outlined the signs of the zodiac, knowing the movements of the heavens.

The Egyptian Adepts were well-informed, well prepared men, tested by the most excruciating means, and the initiates that had come to know themselves, were known as "sons of Ra", and gods among men.

They studied man, his " fearfully and wonderfully " constituted being, mastered the knowledge and use of finer things and veiled all their wondrous wisdom in symbolic form, language, and ritual acts, personifications of things real and imagined, they preserved and protected their venerable arcanum.

The sacred (secret) sciences have been kept, inviolate through the ages, handed down a few true adepts at a time.

## Chapter Fifteen:  The Law of Silence

*" The council of the brotherhood convened....the hierophant exclaimed, why seek for wisdom in the halls of men?"*

This type of question or some variation of it is presented to every potential candidate in practically any sacred school, religious organization, philosophical group, or fraternal order, in some form.

The qualifications for acceptance, usually solicits an agreement to abide by certain conditions, and laws, to practice some customs or traditions and adhere to some doctrine. However, with certain types of groups, especially those that maintain some hallowed aspects of the ancient wisdom, an oath is required to secure conformity and ensure the continuance of that knowledge and practice by which circumspection is indispensable.

Most begin their spiritual journey, philosophical inquires, and mystical experiences without a clear conception, or appreciation for the  trials and test that will most certainly confront them in their quest, but usually express with the greatest confidence, that if allowed to "enter..those dismal crypts", they will of

167

course, " pass the hardest of the test ".

*"....The master said, take then the vow of secret brotherhood..."*

A vow of fidelity, should fully protect by silence and prudence, that which has been placed in one's care, never under any circumstances whatsoever carelessly revealed.

These sacred oaths, the first tests of faithfulness, loyalty and trustworthiness, are found to be broken usually for selfish or self serving purposes, and immediately proves the aspirant unfit beyond any doubt.

It is of great interest how a few, having barely set foot in the Adept Chamber of the Moorish Science Temple, begin to publish materials and information they allege to be adept in nature. While countless others, though not being active in any type temple, organization, or order, faithfully maintain their integrity, and protect the Prophet and the Temple by their obedience.

How is it that so many of our ideological brothers and sisters so conveniently exclude the most fundamental concepts and spiritual tenants of Noble Drew Ali's instructions altogether? He then, that is "unfaithful in the least" is certain to be unfaithful also in more. It's not about religion, religion like the Sabbath, was made to serve man, man was never made to serve any religion.

There are practical reasons as well for the observance of sacred oaths, lest the secrets of holy things, divine knowledge or otherworldly power, fall into devious, dangerous and wicked hands. The willful violation of sacred trust and confidence of our brother men is a self-serving act of betrayal, anyone that would " betray his fellowman just to serve his selfish self, is never a man to trust ".

It is not merely in the significance of some secret words or little known information, but all that it implies, considering the various schools of instructions, their benefits and privileges, strict rules are imposed, not for the exclusive interest of the body, but the benefit and protection of the individual as well.

Paul, a Christine adept, makes expressive mention of a man he knew " whether in the body or out of the body", Paul "could not tell", but does relate how the person by some means ( accidental or purposely is unclear) was " caught up to the third heaven....heard unspeakable words which it is not lawful ( lawful here is used to refer to something that should not be in public) for a man to utter ".

In the days of antiquity, a man being accepted into the sacred mysteries, was a man in peril of his life, initiation was a long and strenuous process, and failure usually left no options, yet by trial, test, "and buffetings of many kind, the student emerges the master of his life and with the true life of a master.

The life and work of true masters resembles the Egyptian statue that personified silence, Harpocrates, which was depicted with enormous eyes, as well as ears, but a small and "tightly shut mouth".

Even from time immemorial, the esoteric masters have thoroughly expressed and defined, the absolute necessity of the rule of discretion in clear and precise terms.

It is here, in this world of things made manifest, that silence, above all, is proven to be golden and the only absolute proof that one truly knows, is that he steadfastly refuses to speak about it.

*" A still tongue, carries a wise head..."*

There are indeed few who know the truth about man,

and that it is foolish to try and impart it to the ignorant.

Thus, there are those who submit to the universal law, that such sacred things belong in the realm of the Holy, and as the sparrow on the house top, they watch and are silent. With such there is no feigned innocence, they shun great honors, and all the accolades of man. There is something that they have learned and learned well, that silence is also invaluable.

Words are the manifestation of thoughts, and, as there is a time and a place, so to speak, for all things, that which is holy finds no place in a world of darkness, neither should that which is sacred ever touch the ground.

A devout and pure heart is but the temporary abode of the spirit of truth, of that which is pure, even Moses removed the shoes from his feet, soiled with the filth of the earth, in the presence of divine Glory.

There is a perfect silence that is natural and it has been said that "God works in silence and nothing but silence can express Him". Those who can see the light, walk in the light, and through the sacred door of silence, enter at will, the eternal splendor of the truth, the purest silence in practice of the holy science, produces the clearest conception and more frequent impartation

171

of the divine wisdom.

The warnings to those who deviate from the path of righteousness are genuine and given that by this we will better understand why one should not public-ally, loosely speak of these things, it is therefore not a silence to be born of fear, but of Holy reverence.

Upon every initial entrance of one upon the mystic path, the law of silence is set in effect and prompted to respond with the measure equivalent to any violation of the Divine laws.

Observation of everyday life should confirm to us that "..he who speaks (often) does not know and he who knows, does not speak" and "a fool is known by the multitude of words".

How often, in the midst of people engaged in a normal conversation, has been heard the voice of the fool, or obviously uninformed person speaking forth words out of place, or has been present when a musician has lost, momentarily, the rhythm of his instrument.

Such things are distinguished quite promptly, the discordant notes, are an assault on the ears of the listeners, and of greater notice than the still harmonious instruments.

All conscious men speak the universal language of silence and circumspection, it is a (posture) as well as a medium, and by it wise men are made wiser and holy men are consecrated.

The rule of silence is the first and far most requirement presented to any inquiring mind, for by this means alone will any 'secret' or mystery be revealed. Of a greater necessity, and more trustworthy guide on the path of enlightenment, a truly life and death undertaking, is that with sincerity, faithfulness, and true humility, shall an aspirant labor toward the increasing light, till immortal life is actualized and life's labors proven not in vain.

The world of the unseen, is a world of indescribable and eternal powers, it is an utter folly therefore, " for smelly culprits with their insidious plans, to try to invade such realms ".

These are reasons why, irregardless of the system or school of instruction, the aspirant is tried and tested, retried and retested, delayed, denied, or diverted if possible, and in many cases intentionally misled, that only the pure in heart will see the king.

All symbolic languages work in conjunction with the symbols themselves, the signs are reserved for those in need of directions to a particular place or location as well as being accurately indicative of that one's actual position or knowledge.

In one light or another it is consistently demonstrated, that " the best things in the hands of a fool may be turned to his own destruction, and out of the worst, the wise, will find means of good ".

## Chapter Sixteen:  The Holy City

*".........Benares is the sacred city of the Brahms, and in Benares Jesus taught.........."*

Benares has been called, even in modern times, India's religious capital and one of the oldest living cities in the world. There exist more than a few references to visits by Jesus the Christ to this sacred site in different religious, historical and esoteric records.

Considered a holy city by the Jain, followers of the Buddhist faith, and the most Holy place on earth in the Hindu tradition, Benares has been a destination for pilgrims for thousands of years.

One of the most archaic and enduring symbols of man's journey into eternity, is his quest to find the eternal city, his original home, made symbolic by the different 'Holy Cities' that dot the face of the earth and the custom in countless geographical locations among vastly differing people of making necessary expeditions, or religious journeys.

Whether the location of the Delphian oracle, the great pyramid plateau of Egypt or the soaring heights of

175

Machu Picchu in Peru, people have always designated
certain locations as holy, sacred, or miraculous.
Places where great prophets or saviors were born,
sages taught, where miracle workers healed, were
great men lived, and where they died.

The holiest city of the Jewish people is the city of
Jerusalem, a city given special status in the religious
laws of Israel.  It is also the holiest site of many
followers of the Christian religion, because of its
connections and significance in the life and teachings,
even the death of Jesus the Christ, on whom their
religion is based. Jerusalem is recognized by Islamic
adherents as the third holiest site in their tradition,
after Mecca and Medina, and it is from Jerusalem,
where it is believed that the Prophet was taken up into
heaven.

Cities like ancient Mecca, the holiest city in Islam,
where not hundreds, but perhaps thousands of years
before the advent of Mohammed, was a center of trade
and exchange of cultural, ideological, philosophical,
and mystical thought.

Many of the tribes of the desert practiced their ancient
alchemical wisdom and held among themselves
knowledge of the Egyptian mysteries, and, as all
people who are of necessity nomadic, they included in
their circuitous routes, traditional, periodic visits to

holy places and sacred shrines.

The making of such a journey, to a sacred shrine, holy city or the like, may hearken to age old rituals and public ceremonies initiated by the ancient priesthood of the mystery systems, as living deposit of their sacred knowledge.

The traveling of the worshipers and devotees, through unseen dangers, hazards, and other terrorizing events, to their spiritual destinations, and there receiving some spiritual gift or blessing, and afterward returning with the prized possession to their places of origin.

The circle, is symbolic also of life, human life, which we ceremoniously perpetuate in repetitive, circular, self-perpetuating fashion, in theory, ensuring continuation. Could the perfect, never ending life, be perfectly ordered concentric periods of existence, like ripples in a pond, ever reaching out to the boundlessness of forever ?

How shall we ascend unto the ideal state, the highest plane of life, and has not wisdom the only eye to perceive it ?

## Chapter Seventeen: The Sword of Justice

*" the peace of society dependeth on justice, the happiness of individuals on the safe enjoyment of all their possessions...No man lives unto himself, for every living thing is bound by cords to every other living thing... and if you touch a fiber of any living thing you send a thrill from the center to the outer bounds of life".*

America's current social atmosphere, its political addiction to public posturing especially, appears to be also the result of outdated, colonial, isolationist thinking.

All across the U.S., many Americans see the game of racism, prejudice, and privileges for what they really are, as well as those persons on both sides of those issues, who profit most by keeping the status quo, by ensuring that things remain the same.

It has been always to our own detriment, that we not see for ourselves and our children a place of actual equal opportunity, American citizenship and standing in these United States, absent any malice, conflict, or prejudicial treatment. Such a place does in fact exist, but it will not, nor can it ever be given or granted.

Freedom is one's own responsibility to appropriate, and to demand respect, the greater responsibility,to defend. It is to be assumed and lived, insisted upon wherever and whenever questioned.

The word karma is derived from an ancient form of the word that denotes 'action', thus, karma is it's self action of any kind.  It is the explication of things that occur with no apparent reason, invisible powers, acting and reacting in the great drama that is human life.

*"...think not bold man because thy punishment has been delayed, that the arm of Allah has weakened, nor flatter thyself with hopes that He winketh at thy doings........"*

A free man has a divine right to peace and personal tranquility, without undue and intrusive aggression from other men, as in the overall unrestricted freedom to go about and transact business unmolested in an open and free society.

Any concerted effort, covert or overt, to abuse or deprive any citizen of the United States of America, of their right to free national citizenship, by name and by principal, is in direct contradiction to fundamental doctrine of the American constitution.

All such persons as are found to be in direct or indirect opposition to the law of the land, whether they be community organized or unorganized, individuals, groups, local, state, federal, agent or employee acting in official capacity, authority, or under "color of law", are subject to the force of law, where fines, penalties, or imprisonment may be imposed in the interest and for the purposes of justice.

It is of dire necessity to encourage our young brothers and sisters that they choose an intelligent path in life and resist the foolish path of hatred and self destruction, neither allow themselves to be entangled in the legal justice system, where literally millions of our young African American men are being herded like cattle into the jails and prisons of the lands.

Marginalized their entire lives, wards of the state, in a vicious cycle of anger, incarceration, disappointments, and confusion. This is a manifestation of the things that Drew Ali may have been talking about, as we can plainly see with the destruction of our people through sin and disobedience.

Our young people, who do not know the history or the intense reality of our struggle here in America, are for all intents and purposes being extrapolated out of the constitutional body, labeled as lawbreakers, outside the law, they are to their absolute disadvantage,

180

classed with all other undesirables, aliens, foreigners, strangers, etc.

Without understanding, countless numbers are being ensnared, not realizing that their violent reactions, and emboldened violations of the law, often will put the sword of justice in the hands of their worst enemies, giving them all the power and authority to take away their peace. He seizes them by the neck and takes control of their actions, garnishes their wages and disrupts their income, finally he puts them in cages and the keys are in his pockets.

It may take years for a young soul to realize, years after justice has run its course, the very perpetrator himself, punished with the knowledge of the truth, as the clouds of ignorance, anger, and confusion, part enough for him to see the light, he was his own worst enemy.

When the conditions that exist in society today are viewed in this context it becomes more apparent why Drew Ali in the "Moorish leader's historical message to America" writes concerning the aims, objects, rules and regulations, of his Moorish Science Temple of America.

The intended inference being that, adherence to the

181

doctrine and understanding the purposes and the principals of the organization, would be the means of causing his people to adhere to the principles of love, truth, peace, freedom, and justice in....."relations with mankind in general".

Further, that the given information would enable the Moorish-Americans, to more clearly see the duty and wisdom of at all times upholding those fundamental principles which are desired for our civilization of our posterity, such as obedience to law, respect and loyalty to government, tolerance and unity.

*"The object of our organization is to help in the great program of uplifting fallen humanity and to teach those things necessary to make our members better citizen".*

Those things which Noble Drew Ali taught  through his doctrine, the long hidden history of the ex-slaves, the glorious history of the people they had descended from, and the mystic knowledge that had inspired civilizations of their ancestors as they led the world for thousands of years, was taught to empower the people to be themselves.
This attitude, new way of thinking, and living had not been known by most of the descendants of Africa since at least 1779.

Over the last 100 years Black people have been able to study their true history, and millions have escaped the burden of slave designations, descriptions, and publicly demanded and defined stereotypes, misrepresentation, and misconceptions by what American society insists is of a Negro, Black, or Colored person. Historians, authors, and script writers have been able to work uncontested to give these public definitions of Black people a false appearance of legitimacy, often twisting grotesquely facts of history, science, even religion, to support the dehumanizing and distorting of the self esteem or sense of worth 'Black people', like every other human being on earth would naturally develop.

Drew Ali therefore explored in essence the only escape for a people outside the law and perpetually subject to all manner of names and abuses and mistreatment s, to elevate them to an equal, undeniable place in the land of their birth, by bringing them out of the darkness into the marvelous light.

*"... And when these principles are violated, justice then must take its course...."* The Omnipotent Judge does not dispense justice according to our whims, neither does He act at our pleasures.

We should always without questioning consider the circumstances without bias and treat all people with respect, consideration, and dignity that every human being deserves.

There may be, in the final analysis, not quite as many as one would think that will subscribe to the institutional and intentional oppression and disenfranchisement of others, perhaps due to some understanding of the nature of justice and divine retribution.

## Chapter Eighteen:  Light of the Word

*" Allah's meeting place with man is in the heart, and in a still small voice he speaks, and he who hears is still. "*

*" Thou man alone canst speak. Wonder at thy glorious prerogative; and pay to Him who gave it to thee a rational and welcome praise, teaching thy children wisdom, instructing the offspring of thy loins in piety... "*

The ever quickening pace of life today, the explosive growth of technology, is being driven by a greater need for better, clearer, instantaneous communication.

Without the word, the articulate sound, that is the audible symbol and expression of a thought, a sound, an idea, thought or the thinking capacity could not develop beyond the level of the animal or conceive of the most basic concepts.

The word is the very point around which our world, each person, and their own unique personal realities, revolves.

If words then are the center of our daily experiences, involving hearing, understanding, and responding, it is

185

therefore imperative that we perfect as far as possible our ability to hear, understand, as well as effectively communicate them.

Any prophet, mystic, adept, sage, philosopher, or religious scholar, can but communicate that transcendent wisdom acquired through practical experience and intuitive knowledge, by symbolic speech or other type of language. Personal gnosis can never be completely communicated to others, in some circumstances it is even unlawful to speak of some things.

The written word, sacred scripture, divine revelations, are given to the world that all men might have access to its light and guidance, written by men, it is as perfect or imperfect as a man, even so, the invisible hand aids in the fulfillment of that purpose.

In the holy and divine instructions, great emphasis is placed on learning to hear, to hear correctly, and clearly, to listen with the inner ear, for the ring of authenticity.

We develop our capacity to think, reason, to comprehend as we exercise our mental faculties, we are unlimited, except, by what we ourselves believe that we can achieve. It takes even the most basic measure of intelligence to survive each day, it is then

186

in our own best interest, to continually seek out and to take advantage of every opportunity to learn, grow, develop, and perfect as far as possible, any useful skill or ability.

A boundless number of thoughts may form, even visions in the mind, yet almost nothing becomes manifest without in some way being communicated by the spoken or written word.
In short, nothing is done until it is said, audibly or inaudibly.

It should command more than a passing interest, that our ability to communicate by the power of the word or at least a universally recognized substitute, serves throughout this existence as a hook, from which the balance of our lives hang.

Our lives may sometimes be an uncomfortable manifestation of our unconsidered, idle, destructive and thoughtlessly uttered, discordant words.

The Holy Scriptures of the different religious or spiritual faith traditions form one great volume of revelation to man, born of that pure doctrine, teaching the absolute power of God, the immortality of life, the brotherhood of all men, and the triumph of light over darkness.

187

The book is itself sometimes viewed as a symbol of the word of truth, the word of God, the true light, that makes visible the path of life for everyone that comes into this world. No book compiled by men can restrict the infinite thoughts, or the boundless mind of God. We have only by His mercy what he has revealed through His holy prophets and messengers.

However as a guide to daily life, the Holy Books, the sacred scriptures, are indispensable, they are the reservoirs of knowledge and learning, the great quarries, from which are drawn every stone which will constitute the eternal temple, the holy house of worship.

The Vedas, Avesta, the great Qur'an of Mecca, even the philosophy of antiquity ascribed to Egyptian dynasties with successive history of thousands of years, have long been reverenced as " the sacred books of the east ", whose light sustained the most advanced knowledge of the invisible realms for unknown ages".

Many of those ancient doctrines, spiritual verities, along with divine revelations concerning mystical illuminations, the divine will, and prophetic dispensations, continue and are recorded in "your Holy Bible", the manifestations of the word in the west.

With the tools of practical knowledge, divine insight,

and harmonious thought, every builder builds in accordance with the divine plan as he receives them for his work, laid out in the volume of book he has found holy and the ideal instructions in life.

We conceive of things to a limited degree, because they exist to a limited degree," as the ether vibrates so and so ", and when the conditions change that actually caused those 'things', they cease to be and disappear. We are all in the process of unfolding in understanding and ability, "as does the bud unfold show the flower".

Ali, a master Adept, in his compilation of the circle seven, appears to provide his students with actual as well as symbolic tools with which the spiritual temple of man is to be built, and employable wisdom, the historical accuracy of which should solicit little concern when viewed in this context.

Simple semantics are usually enough to completely cloud almost every issue, preventing little if any real communication between people, the message sent is rarely the message received, if received at all.

Many of us are eliminated from participation in the larger society, neither are we able to take full advantage of the many privileges of American freedom and citizenship, for the most part because we either do not understand, or lack the intelligence and

189

know how, to take advantage of the opportunities.

We can by no means hope to understand the true nature and purpose of things, of life, of religion, the world or the wisdom that is come down through the ages, until we come to see the basic truth for our selves, learn and practice until we can effectively apply the knowledge of everyday life.

Very often, our personal definitions and the actual definitions of things are vastly and entirely different. Though religion is a highly personal affair, it is often defined by participation in ceremonies, rituals, or adherence to a particular doctrine or belief system. The word 'religion', is derived from the Latin word 'Religio', or the phrase 're-lagare', meaning to bind something back together, giving the implication of something broken being put back together, restored.

Likewise the word scientists, in the modern terminology, refers to investigative fields of research mostly connected with biological, geological, or other physical sciences. But the Moorish scientist is more closely related to them as a meta physician, a type of investigative philosopher, practical psychologist and spiritual practitioner.

Every man or woman, whether they are attentive or inattentive, are provided by divine providence,

190

practical experiences and flashes of insight into the mysteries and hidden things of life, thus a person compiles their own book of proven wisdom, based on their own life's experiences, constituting their own individual cabala, or personally received lessons .

Exercised by meditation, inflection, study, application, concentration and prayer, the heart of man becomes as pliable as the softest clay.

Our worship of God is best accomplished in our developing to be the expression He created us to be, unfolding " as does the bud unfold to show the flower".

All of creation and every living thing, the seen and the unseen, are of variant types of intelligence and spiritual life, and by intelligence and spiritual light are they realized. Therefore is one capable of perceiving that which they are prepared to perceive, understanding what one is prepared to understand, experiencing likewise what one is prepared to experience.

The human being is given wide latitude in the exercise of his freedom, yet does one also bear the responsibility that is added to it by Divine discretion.

From yonder realms or higher planes of life, so the

191

immortal drama of the great humanity unfolds, the wisest among us working to ensure a continuous emergence of consciousness.

It may come as a shock to some or to the dismay of others that there is no religion, at least not in the earthly sense with which we are most familiar, on the higher planes of life. Another definition of the word religion can be taken from its French and Latin origins, where the word denotes the repairing or "binding back" together something that has been broken, or otherwise separated.

In this instance, it is the idea of a restored relationship, a return of man to his actual place of birth, where religion becomes factual rather than theoretical. Learning there, is as the mystical experience here, or divine illumination, interpreted in the context of each person's spiritual, theological, psychological and philosophical orientation.

These things are extra ordinary, and can present a great ordeal of emotional and psychological difficulty, is best to agree to that which we know is right, and reverence the majesty of the omnipotent.

Is it not here in this world, this earth realm, that we face this most difficult test of living? And afterward, shall we not reach fruition, shall we not then be

completely what we know, absolute certainty that man
is an immortal being?

## Chapter Nineteen: The Third Resurrection

*" The sons of men are toiling hard on desert plains, and burning sands and rocky soils, are doing what their fathers did, not dreaming they can do aught else. Behold a master comes, and tells them of a hidden wealth..... And Jesus opened up the way...."*

*"They put me in a tomb, and then I wrestled with the conqueror of men. I conquered death, I stamped upon him and arose. Brought immortality to light and painted on the walls of time a rainbow for the sons of men, and what I did all men shall do..."*

*" Know thyself, and the pride of His creation, the line uniting divinity and matter; behold a part of Allah Himself within thee....."*

That, was the primary science, that sustained, enabled, and encouraged all of the monumental endeavors which were undertaken and accomplished by the great civilizations of antiquity, the science of man, the knowledge of his being, the earnest inquiry into his purpose, the animation and indubitable use of his latent potentials.

It is a science learned through living, through being, as a human, that which you are of necessity being at that particular time or for certain purposes. As important as what we are, is where we are, and why, for one is always certain to " find one's self where he can solve his problems best".

The scientist of life, sometimes compare phenomena in the terms of microcosmic, as it relates to human beings, or as macro-cosmic, in reference to the universal manifestation of universal life in totality, the diametric extreme.

But man himself, is not the body nor the soul, he is a spirit and a part of his Creator, the whole animating life force of the universe, of everything that was, is, or evermore to be.

Untold thousands if not millions of years, have the sons of men dwelt on these lower planes of life, and the work of great master-men, is to help restore that which was lost, the consciousness of Holy Breath, the knowledge that God (Allah), and man are one, that in the flesh of man there is the essence of the resurrection of the dead.

*"This essence, quickened by Holy Breath, can raise the ethers to a higher tone, and make them like the ethers above, which human eyes cannot behold.."*

195

The word resurrection has Latin and Old French origins, and literally means," to rise again ", it also carries the implication of rising from the dead and coming back to life.

In some form or another, by some means and through what ever necessary process, we find this three-fold cycle in all the ways of this life, as birth, duration, death and birth again.

We may have seldom considered it, but each of us re-enact that cycle everyday of our lives, being born anew every morning, living out our days conducting our affairs, engaging in our endeavors, and as we lay asleep at night it is a gift of the Father-God that we do not sleep the sleep of death.

On every occasion that the will of man and will of the All-Mighty-God are one, the resurrection is a demonstrated, actualized fact. Our human lives, are wholly given to us, that we may labor to bring our wills in tune with the Deific Will.

*" Man will regain his lost estate, his heritage, but he must do it in a conflict that cannot be told in words".* This great drama of human rebirth, renewal, and transformation has been illustrated throughout history in the various rites of baptismal death, burial, and

resurrection, or the familiar initiation and raising
ceremonies.

In practically every true and divine religion ever
practiced on earth, has been the hope and some
tangible demonstration of divine assurance in this
present life, and immortality in the life to come.

In the initiatory schools, ancient as well as
contemporary, the upwardly spirialic cycles of
elevation, information, and 'insight', by measure, step,
or degree, included in the most of them, a ritualistic
death, burial, and resurrection of the initiate into the
school or order's " light " or sacred wisdom.

The result desired of illumination, is the spiritual
confirmation of the corporeal instructions that have
been actualized in the life and consciousness of the
individual, therefore, sincerity serves it's master
faithfully.

Among Freemasons of western tradition, by the three
step process, initiate to master, they are made sons of
the widow and masters of the craft, free to travel and
build and to receive fair wages and just compensation.

The adepts and Moorish scientists use the god-man
paradigm, and the allegorically instructive birth, death,
and resurrection of love and light made manifest, to

extricate the sacred doctrine for analytical study and practical experimentation.

In the Khametian mystery system, the successful adept endured the spiritual process called " the coming forth by day" or into the presence of the gods of Egypt, and the knowledge of the arcane wisdom. From those sacred schools down to the present era, the initiates of a multitude of "houses of wisdom" that have drawn their secret knowledge and hidden wisdom from the shrine of Mother Africa, have stepped forth onto the mystic path.

From the most remote regions of the earth, to the densest jungles of tropical South America or equatorial Africa, vastly differing societies initiate their adolescents into adulthood with some variation of a ceremonial death and rebirth into a "greater" life.

Those more observant ones are always apt to see immediately beyond any ceremonial, ritualistic, or other symbolism and intuitively perceive the esoteric assertions, such will usually have a predisposition to spiritual things, and if uncorrupted by the world, are the most patient, effective and enduring builders.

The actual philosophic death, is a burial in psychological obscurity, a turning within, dying to the world, reversing the order of priorities.

The philosophical contemplation of life is where the ideas evolving into unique ideologies, and to some extent our purest religious or spiritual perceptions are synthesized into an absolute, on man's highest level of thought and life.

Quite the contrast to the life of the unconscious, those in a state of spiritual, intellectual, or moral darkness, the subsequent mental and spiritual deficiencies, that create for such as those, an almost impossible condition for any human being to live in.

Constant overwhelming frustration, as one fights through life for survival, against hostile forces, and hidden adversaries, buffeted and attacked from every side, ignorant of the way of this entanglement, or escape from the unrelenting difficulties and adverse circumstances.

The key of life, of death and of the resurrection of the dead, may be understood and rightly applied as moral, philosophical, as well as spiritual ideas.

It appears universal, that as a man, or society, and nation for that matter, with conscious intent and effort advances toward the true light, even so is that transformation process initiated, man is thus transfigured by the light that he sees.

In the third resurrection, the Moors rise, looking like a nation, a new people, and thoroughly American, by which is meant, that the essential ideas of freedom, justice, and equality, are finally personified in a people who historically have been denied those fundamental rights, and accept that they themselves are the answer to their own dilemma as well as America's best hope for the future.

# Chapter Twenty :   Working in the Light

Even before one can receive any degree, any measure, of spiritual insight, or divine illumination, it should be sincerely considered, that one must have the light before they can receive the light.

Light is a very interesting phenomena as well as instructive symbol, light, that allows us to see what would otherwise be obscure and invisible to us.

Darkness must always give way to light, darkness is the antithesis or direct opposite of light. It is easy to understand one by the clear comprehension of the other.

When infused with divine wisdom and immersed in the marvelous light, you see clearly what is possible. Because many have believed the possible, just believing and going forward in light of the knowledge that they had, they succeeded. There is only one divine way, that is the way of truth, of light, the way of positive energy in motion.

For those, there is no darkness as such, because, the light by its means illuminates all dark places, in its manner making even the darkness visible, perceptible, or comprehend-able. Neither should we purposely turn

201

down dark avenues, lest we be tempted or entangled and our lights grow dim, or worse, be put out.

In the life of a regenerated being, having been transformed by a systematic process or divine intervention, all divergent streams of thought flow into one complete personality, who by the light of an enlightened consciousness advances into eternity.

This may be why, a strong, stable, solid earthly foundation is strongly recommended, as being so vitally important to the exploration of alternative realities, of mystical experiences and divine illumination.

## Chapter Twenty One: The Gold that Rules

Respect, usually implies a careful evaluation or estimation of the worth of a person or thing and of the measure of recognition that is due him or it; often, when the person or thing is esteemed highly, respect implies a show of deference or veneration.

Mutual respect and reciprocal obligations are immovable parts of the foundation of any enlightened society, when the minds of all the populace turn ultimately toward its overall good, that society will prosper, that nation will be the leader among nations. Respect, is people giving their best out of a sense of duty, and rightfully expecting the same in return.

There is a golden thread, that permeates the entire fabric of all the mystery systems, past and present, teaching the esoteric wisdom of the secret doctrine. The contemplation and intuitive comprehension of abstract concepts and realities, the science behind the teaching of immortality, the mystical forays into divine illumination, and the communication of all things by symbolic methods.

## Chapter Twenty Two:   His Nobelist Image

*"...Moors are men, upright, independent, and fearless, who follow their prophet to a destiny that is neither unknown nor uncertain, they are fortified by an impregnable doctrine built upon love, truth, peace, freedom and justice.*

*The principles of love, truth, peace, and freedom, when faithfully adhered to, are strong enough to meet the requirements of any reasonable law, and when such principles are violated, justice then  must take its course..."*

Men are men because they have matured enough to both understand and exercise principles, this requires the knowledge
of one's self, spiritual mastery over one's self, a man among men, a child before the Everlasting.

Human beings have long and in various teachings been regarded as having been created in the image of God. By some means, humanity separated or fell from that original design, and the purpose of all true and divine teachings, religions, or alternative instruction and training, is to restore man to his proper place.

In the Hindu religion, the true self, the Atman, the unchangeable, is a manifestation of alternate reality, of god, the life of every person, in Egyptian theology it was the body of light, the final state of man.

Most do not live today in the true image of the divine, but are enslaved, to the distorted image, and do not know who they are or who their Father-God is.

To but the most unlearned and profane among the unequaled people of Khamet, was the Sun the direct object of worship, indeed their reservoir of esoteric wisdom suggests that their religion in essence, to be the goal of imitating the Sun, immortality for the one, like the deity Ra, becomes the Sun.

## Chapter Twenty Three:  The Dome of Purity in Life

Purity in life, is purity in action, manifesting it's invigorating influence, as a Sun's vivifying rays in its sphere of influence.

The East has been long symbolic of the place where light, understanding, consciousness and spiritual illumination,  the precious jewels of wisdom, are to be found.

Any man is a prince who rules well the kingdom of his own life over which he has been given decisive authority.

One is considered wise who clearly discerns conditions, situations, or persons, and consistently makes the appropriate determinations.

Wisdom is of course acquired through countless trials, difficulties, and circumstances, and even with the best use of our time, resources, and the good counsel of our peers, will we arrive at the knowledge of the truth?

*" Hear now, oh everything that is, was, or evermore will be, for Wisdom speaks from the highest plane of*

*spirit life. Man is a thought of Allah, all thoughts of Allah are infinite; they are not measured up by time, for things concerned with time, begin and end..."*

We study all type of religions philosophies, contemporary thought, sciences, mysticism and religions of the world, with hopes of gaining a better understanding of ourselves, and those around us, of life, the nature of creation, and the boundlessness of time and space.

*"...without a foe a soldier never knows his strength, and thought must be developed by the exercise of strength..."*

*"..Is there anything in which thy weakness appears more than in our desiring of things? It is in the possessing and the using of them, good things cease to be good in our enjoyment of them, but "that which permanently delighteth must be permanent ".*

In the mundane world, opposites quite easily attract and the conflict is the natural outcome, yet in the life that is to come such conflicts are unknown.

All the sons of light must be the operative, visible examples of purity in life, of industriousness, of the highest ideas as expressed in the purest teachings of the divine wisdom available among the sons of men.

## Chapter Twenty Four:   The Prince of Peace

*" the door to the banquet hall was in the East, a
vacant chair was at the table to the East.....a stranger
entered unannounced, and raising up his hands in
benediction said, " All Hail ", a halo rested on his
head and light unlike the light of sun, filled all the
room..."*

For men of light, insight, and the prudent path of life,
wisdom is indeed the principle and prerequisite to all
intentions and endeavors.

One is considered wise, who effectively discerns
persons, conditions, or situations and consistently
makes the proper decisions concerning whatever may
be the issue at hand.

Wisdom is most often acquired with great difficulty,
through countless events, trial's, tests, hardships and
circumstances.

Which affects our power or ability to make the best
use of our time, energy, resources, and the good
counsel of others

Every man is a prince that rules well the kingdom of his own life over which he has been granted authority and recognizes with the eyes of soul the "daystar from on high".

*"......and Jesus said; " my brother man your thoughts are wrong; your heaven is not far away, is not a country to be reached; it is a state of mind....."*

Wrong actions are the result of wrong thinking, they are the manifest of concentrated thoughts and the work of one's imaginative powers.  Thoughts of other thinking things, the thoughts, acts, and deeds of man, for better or worse influence the atmosphere in which we all must live.

The great work of all masterminds, is to influence for good, the thoughts and higher possibilities of all our fellow human beings.

Taking every opportunity to lift the human family and assist them toward that divine image in which we are best suited to be ourselves.

All men desire at heart, freedom, justice, and equality, the blessed state of peace within, tranquility without.

The crude religions of the primitive world, with the
waring and often human-like gods and goddesses of
the ignorant masses, were the only tools available to
raise the consciousness, or bring order out of chaos
in those days of gross superstition, and spiritual
darkness.

Without any special regard to a particular group, body,
order or organization, any people, that are a sincere,
committed part of that " great work of uplifting fallen
humanity ", assumes thereby the individual and
collective duty, the spiritual work of all builders, to
extract from those instructions and directives that
essential, life-giving doctrine.

# Chapter Twenty-Five: The Daystars from on High

*"...We call these sons revealers of the Light, but they must have the light, before they can receive the Light...."*

*" The problem of the age has been solved; a son of man has risen from the dead, has shown that human flesh can be transformed...and so, I am , the message that I bring to you.."*

Here is reference to that which life is spent to build, even so, the work is not ending, but beginning, for it is at this point that we are best prepared to begin.

*"The wise man cultivates his mind with knowledge, the improvement of the arts is his delight and their utility to the public crowneth him with honor."*

Likewise, he fully understands that all, true worshipers worship the one All-mighty Creator, the true and ever living-God, but all do not see Him alike. Many people name or identify with only the part of the Father that they can comprehend, and this to them is all of God. Therefore, for such persons, their idea is their God, or the only type of God that they can imagine and accept.

Millions of people continue to sit on the sidelines of life, hopeless, in the very land of opportunity, marginalized, living an American nightmare, while praying for the American dream.

Thought must be developed, the mind must be exercised in the use of its different faculties, resistance builds strength, endurance, and perseverance yields the object.

Speculative thought gives birth to a multitude of theoretical inferences and postulations, an ever evolving proliferation of half-truths, usually accepted before the actual facts are firmly established. While impartial observation, earnest and sincere inquiry yields slow, but gradual degrees of insight.

In ordinary scientific inquiry, the bodies of knowledge are established on certain known, observable facts, which, dictate that additional research travels along theoretical lines.

In the practice of the divine sciences however, abstract ideas, are the very means of establishing to each individual one's satisfaction, the very desirable facts themselves.

*" weak and ignorant as thou art, o child of the dust,*

*humble as thou oughtest to be, wouldst thou raise thy thoughts to infinite wisdom? Wouldest thou see omnipotence displayed before thee? Contemplate thine frame."*

By all means avoid foolishness, pride, and conceit, they are three deadly peaks, from which countless numbers fall to ruin from those precipitous heights.

They often appear, dis-appear, then, reappear again throughout the pages of history, extra-ordinary men, men of re-noun, teachers, lawgivers, builders of great kingdoms and dynasties, the hero of legends, the demigods of mythology, sages, and wise men, an unbroken chain, that disappears into the mists of antiquity.

Since olden times the royal councils of silent brotherhoods have met to contemplate the wisdom of the ages and perfect the practice of the sacred sciences .

The major problems to be solved were death, immortality, the worship of God, and the fellowship of men. The holy brotherhoods of old have long held the keys to those sacred mysteries, and thus the secret doctrine of all the holy men of antiquity was ever protected, transmitted, concealed, hidden under the

214

shadow of signs, symbols and hieroglyphs.

The true and divine prophets, messengers, and
teachers, each to their respective regions and people
sent as revealers of the divine wisdom, yet even then
in simplest forms, in parables, myths, and allegorical
lessons. Such was the doctrine of the Christ and his
parable of  " the pearl of great price ", the Buddha and
the eightfold path,  Mohammed and the revelation,
more specifically the restoration to Arabia the
knowledge of the one and true God,  Zoroaster with
the mysterious forces of light and powers of darkness,
even the Holy law of Moses, symbolized and instituted
in the Pentateuch and tabernacle of the living God.

Yet this great light of life is the heritage, the life, the
light for all men.

The key to opening the doors of insight, is the
application of that infinite wisdom, down through the
ages, alternately lost and then rediscovered, ever
reborn in the life, works, and teachings of some
prophet, mystic, master, or sage. Thus, has that
impregnable doctrine been disseminated throughout
the ages, in different forms, by different traditions,
always embodying the same essence.


Those who have passed down to us this sacred

wisdom, not in historical literature alone, for a true messenger, and emissary of the Holy realm , is certain to " leave his footprints clearly cut, that all can see and be assured that he, their master, went that way ".

Knowing that " man causes his own conditions ", not to mention his oft thoughtless effects in the lives of others, we should therefore the more consciously choose, and purpose from within to be, to exist, to manifest as the sons of the "marvelous light", as builders, workers in the kingdom of light.

The " Moorish fez ", should be of interest to all travelers on the ancient paths, it is the headdress of the consummate mystic and scholar, a master, an adept in the " royal art ", one who has mastered many subjects; knowledgeable, learned, a complete, a total man.

Black is the color of depth as well as mystical death, the mufti verifies the universal law and is attentive to its maintenance and operation.

The fez is a symbol of absolute devotion, a life dedicated to scientific, meticulous investigation into the mysteries of nature, and the only true God.

As the old Moors used to say, "A monkey can wear a fez, but he can't demonstrate it."

It would be utter foolishness to reveal more than what is already public knowledge concerning any adept knowledge or " secrets ", in general or the AC of the MST of A in particular. Suffice it to say that it is far more than any ideological, philosophical, or theological concept to be debated or scrutinized by common persons equipped with only a basic textual familiarity of the subjects.

Therefore, much of the commentary on the subject and content of the AC/MST/A is from person's who are not actually adepts, or worse unfaithful Moors with misconceptions as to what the movement is dedicated to, not true Moorish adepts, active members or not, true Moors, will protect the Prophet.

The greater mysteries were never revealed until the aspiring adept had proven his proficiency and more importantly his faithfulness. The Glory and awesomeness of Majesty, being more than enough reason, that the mystic resolves to forever hold his tongue.

Donning the fez, is a calculated crossing of the mystical bridge to the other side of life, into the world of the eternal, the holy silence, the boundless life. For some western orders such as the Shriners...grotto, etc., it represents forays into eastern philosophy, science and religion.

217

Because of the clear and direct relationships of African American masons to the actual history, rituals, philosophical concepts and especially the regalia of the "mystic shrine", literally the clothes off of the backs of the American Black man's direct ancestors. For those early Black Shriners, a few decades removed from slavery, their experience was usually more solemn and heart felt.

*"Reflection is of the business of man..."*

Reflecting now, on our first unsteady steps, our obscure vision, the faint outline, glimpses of the blazing star of truth, faint even as it was, for then we saw " through a glass darkly ".
Now, with the glow of eternal truth in sight and prudently imparted to us, having come down through the ages, imparted by those divine lessons with which we have been intrusted, now a storehouse of the ancient wisdom.

We are directed to labor, but not for ourselves alone, to work in sincerity and truth, in simple faith, with and for the improvement of our fellow man.

Neither have we been given any good without its admixture of evil, but also the means and the responsibility of throwing off the evil from it.

All to crush the shadow under our feet, tame the lower nature, and to condition the vehicle of power to our divine use and purposes.

The wild beast of nature is subdued by the higher will, by consciously exercising reason and dominion of the intelligent being and put to good use as "the ignoble beast of burden", now obeying the will of the higher-self.

Man, when free of the prison bars of the flesh, is no longer bound and frustrated with evil tendencies, impulses and desires of the carnal nature.

Only a practical rather than a theological knowledge of that which "informs our clay", will enable us to advance onward toward perfection.

All of us, Moorish especially, should daily consider what is required of us, in helping to uplift our own people and our fellow man.

# Concluding Thoughts

We give honor and much encouragement to all of the Moorish-Americans in the iron furnace, you Moors will always be the vanguards of the Movement. Use your situation to assist the Prophet, and do not waste your valuable time.

Understand Moors, that one is "sure to find himself where he can solve his problems best".

Petition for more access to computer information technology, and build up your knowledge base, take advantage of every opportunity to cultivate your mind with knowledge.

From the days when Drew Ali was incarcerated in Chicago, the Moorish law has been plumbed in the institutions all across this country, often the first exposure some have to the knowledge of the truth.

You Moors may have a significant impact on the determinations of the younger generations, if you can be prepared and available to assist even a few of the hordes of young, unconscious Moorish brothers that are flooding the institutions of America in record numbers, into knowledge of Allah, into knowledge of self, into the marvelous light of Ali.

We sincerely thank and appreciate all who have found this work even worthy of consideration, and pray our Father-God, they are the more committed to contributing , in any measure possible, to the great work of uplifting fallen humanity among this Asiatic race and nation.

*" Come all ye Asiatics "*

Peace

## Matheno's Lessons: Fruition

Is there anything more powerful, or anything more insistent, is there anything more revealing than the idea whose time has come? Though delayed, it presses, though undesired it persists. As the traveler is sure of the road before him, or the planter his yet unrealized harvest, so is he who has hope in an unseen promise.

What little faith will sustain it, yet how long the patience that brings it to pass. Obstacles, while powerful to the senses cannot conquer the heart that silently trusts that it shall be.

Learn this, oh man, that the greatest victories are not won by the tongue, neither will the strongest arm most certainly prevail. But the spirit of thy most noble self, unseen, doth secure to thee that thing thou wouldest.

In the eye within it may be first seen, determinations unperceived may give it birth, but truly in the creative essence of thine own heart did it spring forth. Take heed to what is set before the eyes and guard thine ears against ungodliness, so shall thy lessen unpleasant surprises.

# Bibliography

Ali, Noble Drew

The Holy Koran of the Moorish Science Temple of America, 1927

Koran Questions for Moorish Children

Bobo, Jacqueline

The Black Studies Reader

Hudley, Cynthia and Michel, Claudine

Moorish Literature, 1902

Davidson, Basil

The Lost Cities of Africa revised edition, 1970

Dewey, Melvil and Bowker R.R.

The Library Journal 1878

Dowling, Levi H.

The Aquarian Gospel of Jesus the Christ 13th printing, 1964

Durant, Will

Our Oriental Heritage 26th printing, 1963

The Age of Faith 1950

Evans, Harold

The American Century

Fellows, John

An Exposition of The Mysteries

Fort, George Franklin                 Early History and Antiquities,
                                      1881

Gramillion, Zachary                   African origins of
                                      Freemasonry


Greeley, Horace                       The GreatConspiracy, 1885

Hall, Manly P.                        The Secret Teachings of All
                                      Ages
                                      2007 Wilder Publications

James, George G.M.                    Stolen Legacy,  2009
                                      1st printing

Jung, C.C.                            Two Essays on Analytical
                                                Psychology
                                      Princeton University press
                                      1970. second edition, second
                                      printing

Klotter, John C.  and                 Constitutional Law
Kanovitz                              sixth edition, 1991

Knoff, Alfred A.                      The Tree of Culture
                                      New York: 1956

Marden, Orison Swett and              The Consolidated Library,
Devitt, George R.                     1907

Masutani, Fumio                       A Comparative Study of
                                      Buddhism   and Christianity
                                      Tokyo, 1967. 10th edition

225

Merriam Co, G & C                    Webster's Dictionary of
                                     Synonyms 1st edition, 1951

Moore, Keith                         Moorish Circle Seven  2005

Mudie, Robert                        The Surveyor, Engineer and
                                     Architect for the year 1841

Nance, Susan                         Mystery of the Moorish
                                     Science Temple

Nelson Tomas Inc.                    The Holy Bible  1984, 1977

Macoy, Robert and                    General History, Cyclopedia
Oliver, George                       and Dictionary of
                                     Freemasonry

Pike, Albert                         Morals and Dogma

Robertson, John M.                   A Short History of Free
                                     Thought, 1899

Scott, S.P.                          History of the Moorish
                                     Empire in Europe, 1904

Sedgwick, William T. and             A Short History of Science
Schuster, Simon                      1917
                                     Webster's New World
                                     Dictionary
                                     2nd concise edition 1982

Spangler, David                      The Laws of Manifestation

Swain, Joseph Ward                   The Ancient World 1950

The Reader's Digest
Association Inc.

The World's Last Mysteries

Webster-Merriam  Inc.

New Complete Thesaurus

Wright, Charles Alan

Handbook of the Law of
Federal Courts
second edition 1970